W9-CPE-825

SHIP-TO-STOCK

STOCK

An Alternative to Incoming Inspection

Richard J. Laford

ASQC Quality Press
American Society for Quality Control
310 West Wisconsin Avenue
Milwaukee, Wisconsin 53203

Published by

 ASQC Quality Press
• Milwaukee •

Ship-to-Stock
An Alternative to Incoming Inspection

Laford, Richard J.

ISBN 0-87389-017-5

Dedication

To my parents, who taught me to do my best in each task attempted. It is this philosophy that forms the basis for Ship-to-Stock.

Contents

Contents

Page

Figures

Page

Preface

As industry continues to develop progressive manufacturing systems and processes, quality and reliability in all manufactured products are increasingly emphasized. Monitoring that quality and reliability must progress also. Ship-to-Stock is one such monitoring method.

Ship-to-Stock is a comprehensive supplier assessment program which is based on either audits of the supplier, or on the supplier's statistical process controls, or both. Ship-to-Stock departs from the traditional approach to supplier quality — that is, the incoming inspection of all products to ensure conformance to contractual requirements — to a partnership approach that emphasizes a qualified trust in a supplier and the supplier's ability to produce products that are fit for use.

The methodology outlined in this text is not a magic cookbook or canned program that fixes all evils in one easy lesson. Rather it is presented in universal terms which the supplier or customer can modify to meet the particular climate or culture of one's industry or company. The book also gives many examples of the most used mechanics of programs with which the author has come in contact.

The author will strive to establish a uniform Ship-to-Stock Program since it has been the author's experience that many variations of one concept can be very confusing. The reader will note that Ship-to-Stock is a method of verifying that a good total quality control system is in place and is adhered to; therefore, the methodology outlined here will help the reader to identify, qualify and monitor products on a Ship-to-Stock program. It will also stress the cost analysis methods to measure savings and cost avoidance upon which management reporting is based.

The Ship-to-Stock Program should not be considered an entity in itself but one of several integrated factors, many of which are the forerunners of Just-In-Time procurement.

For the author to include his individual debt to those who have influenced this book, he would have to list scores of quality control associates in his own company and many colleagues in other companies, in universities, and in the American Society for Quality Control. A particular debt is owed to Janet Fotos who has assisted the author in the technical writing of this book and other publications, and Philip Fotos for his art work and illustrations used in this and many other works by the author.

Special appreciation must be given to the members of the American Society for Quality Control's Vendor-Vendee Technical Committee and Quality Audit Committee who sponsored the book and continually acted as a sounding board over the past several years for the concepts expressed in this book.

Richard J. Laford

1

Introduction

Ship-to-Stock, loosely defined, is moving a supplier's products directly from your receiving dock to your stock room or manufacturing line for immediate use. Ship-to-Stock is a result of a sound, strictly adhered to management system, combined with a management attitude which understands that effective quality systems can be the prime contributor to product acceptance and fitness for use.

Based on this premise, Ship-to-Stock does not build a quality system. To implement Ship-to-Stock, an adequate quality system is a given; a starting point for both the customer and the supplier.

In addition to an adequate quality system on the supplier side, an adequate quality cost reporting system is necessary on the customer's side. This reporting system should, at least, track and report material acquisition costs and identify inspection times in Pareto form. The customer's supplier survey and audit systems will naturally develop as Ship-to-Stock is begun. The procedures for new product development will be greatly enhanced. This is especially true for design, manufacturability and inspectability review, classifications of characteristics, first article inspection/test and process approval, etc. All of these lead to an effective liaison between the customer and the supplier.

In addition to the supplier having an adequate quality system, Ship-to-Stock emphasizes controls during the supplier's manufacturing process. The areas of lot control and traceability, work and inspection instructions, statistical process control and shipping audits will be enhanced.

After you have ensured the procurement of quality products, the natural result is the ability to receive products and ship them directly to the stock room or production line, therefore avoiding all of the costs which are inherent to regular redundant incoming inspection.

Carrying the above concept further is to ship the products Just-in-Time. With both Ship-to-Stock and Just-in-Time in place, then, and only then, are you truly able to successfully compete in the world market with low cost and, most important, high quality. Certainly a company with these systems in place will survive in an era of World-Class Quality.

2

Ship-to-Stock Methodology

I. CHOOSING THE SUPPLIER AND THE PRODUCT

Once the decision has been made to implement a Ship-to-Stock Program, you must begin by reviewing your current supplier base and determining which suppliers are best suited to the program. Several criteria, helpful to determine suitable suppliers, are discussed here.

Incoming Acceptance History

First, review the incoming quality level of each supplier and his products. Suppliers and parts should always be reviewed on a one-to-one basis since you will want to be able to concentrate on the *specific process* used by the supplier to make *one* specific part or part type. Sometimes, suppliers can manufacture one part or part type with consistent high quality while a second part or part type may be troublesome or less consistent; therefore, the supplier may qualify to ship to stock one part or part type and not another.

As you review your suppliers, a few of them will immediately come to mind due to their consistent acceptability and excellent conformance at incoming. These are the suppliers to look at first since they have already proven that they can make a good, quality part. To qualify them for the Ship-to-Stock Program, you just have to ensure that they can maintain that quality if regular incoming inspection is eliminated.

With the Ship-to-Stock philosophy everyone benefits, you get consistent quality parts and your suppliers can concentrate on the specific part(s) for which they are qualified. As you begin to work with a supplier on one part, you may find the quality of other parts improving. This is an added benefit of Ship-to-Stock and will help you qualify additional parts from your suppliers.

Supplier Survey History

Review any procurement business or quality surveys that have been performed. (Examples of quality and procurement surveys can be found in Appendix C.) You will want assurance that the supplier has a capable, established organization that can ensure product quality, and that the supplier has an effective management organization with well defined quality functions and responsibilities. Always keep in mind the type of business that you are reviewing. Some small ''job shops'' seem to have an informal quality organization or an ill-defined management system; yet, their quality sometimes proves to be far superior to large, less flexible organizations.

Benefit Analysis

Starting with a few suppliers that may be good candidates for the program, you should perform some analysis to determine whether working toward Ship-to-Stock with these suppliers will be functionally beneficial. The STS Checklist (Figure 1) can be used to perform an analysis of a supplier. An initial benefit analysis should include the following points.

- How frequently does the part change?
- Are there any known future changes to the part that the supplier should know about before committing to the program?
- Is the product being produced from stable production tooling, etc.?
- How frequently is the part bought and does it have sufficient inventory requirements?
- Could the part be easily tracked through the production process to facilitate any required purges or corrective actions?
- Is the supplier on a similar program with other companies?

SHIP-TO-STOCK CHECKLIST

Submitted by: _____ Ext. _____

Proposed supplier: _____ Date _____

Proposed part/product: _____

Supplier rating for part/product: _____

If component, is part on the qualified supplier list?   Yes _____   No _____

Can part be traced through the customer's manufacturing process? Explain.

_____

_____

How often is the part bought? What is the average lot size?_____

_____

_____

Cost benefit analysis showing any cost savings/avoidance by shipping this product to stock. (Show method of evaluation on attached sheet.)_____

_____

_____

_____

Briefly describe the ECO activity for this part/product. _____

_____

_____

_____

Is the supplier currently shipping products to other companies under a similar program? If yes, explain. _____

_____

_____

_____

List any other reasons why you feel that this supplier should become a candidate for the STS program. _____

_____

_____

_____

What are R&D's plans for modification or changes to this part? _____

_____

_____

_____

List any other suppliers currently supplying this part. _____

_____

_____

_____

_____

Figure 1

Following the functional analysis, one should do a rough cost/benefit analysis. The cost/benefit analysis will determine the anticipated cost savings and/or cost avoidances. The most common analysis is an accounting approach which basically accounts for the saved material acquisition costs minus the cost to establish and monitor the Program. This is amplified in Appendix B.

An alternative approach is the Dr. W. Edwards Deming "zero incoming inspection versus 100 percent inspection" analysis found in his book *Quality*, *Productivity and Competitive Position*. Dr. Deming proved mathematically that it is cheaper to *not* inspect some parts at incoming when they, if nonconforming, can be easily found and replaced during the manufacturing process. This is the basic premise for a program like Ship-to-Stock, which takes into consideration inventory and inspection requirements, and material movement and labor costs.

If the preliminary research indicates that the supplier is a good quality risk but that annual requirements are low or purchases infrequent, a skip-lot inspection program may be considered as an alternative to normal sample inspection. You may also want to consider statistical alternatives, such as supplier control charting, if the part's conformance is critical to the performance of your own product.

If the supplier compares favorably with all of the above considerations and still looks like a good candidate for the program, then an STS contract and part specification review should be performed.

II.   CONTRACT AND SPECIFICATION REVIEW

The most important aspect of Ship-to-Stock as well as successful supplier-customer relations is communication. In today's world, the primary communication tool is the engineering drawing or specification to which the supplier must adhere via the purchase order.

Before you can successfully qualify specific parts for the Ship-to-Stock Program, the product specifications must be clearly defined by the customer and fully understood by the supplier. This is not the time to play a guessing game between the customer and the supplier, nor should there be any informal exceptions to the specifications. As in many manufacturing environments, the product either must conform to the specification, or the specification must be changed to define the acceptable product. Your specifications must be stable and complete before any consideration of this program since Ship-to-Stock requires strict conformance to specifications.

III.   INITIAL SUPPLIER MEETING

Up to this point, communications with the supplier have only implied the possibility of the Ship-to-Stock Program, but have never formally discussed what Ship-to-Stock really is and how it would affect the supplier. At the initial meeting between the supplier and the customer, the real purpose of the program must be explained to the supplier which is, of course, to ensure on time delivery of conforming products and to save money. One of the motivating by-products of the program is to facilitate greater revenues for the supplier by being a "preferred" supplier.

The initial meeting is the time to describe the goals and philosophies of the Ship-to-Stock Program, the details of the supplier surveys and audits, the consecutive lot inspections and first article inspections and the maintenance required to run the program.

Fully advise the supplier concerning the work that is involved with starting the program and the rewards that can be expected once the supplier is an STS-qualified supplier. Above all, do not promise what the buyer cannot guarantee. It is important to include purchasing personnel in discussions about the program since only they can commit the company's dollars.

During this meeting, an important function that you must perform is listening to the supplier. Listen and understand the supplier's strong points and weaknesses, and exactly what the supplier is willing to do for the program. Since the program does require work and commitment, you will eventually want to reach agreement with the supplier concerning the responsibilities that each of you will have in order to establish and maintain the program.

Ask all of the necessary questions. Listen to and understand the supplier's answers. The supplier will also have many questions, especially if Ship-to-Stock philosophy is new to the supplier. Answer carefully and clearly. Any misunderstanding at this point could create costly problems later on. Above all, be professional. The initial meeting could be the most important step in selling the Ship-to-Stock philosophy to your suppliers. The supplier will need to know that you are willing to stand behind your commitments and you will expect him to stand behind his commitments.

The supplier survey is the next step in the STS Program. You may, if agreeable, perform the survey immediately following the initial meeting or schedule the survey for a later date.

Before we discuss any more particulars concerning the qualification and approval of STS suppliers, we should consider the responsibilities of the Supplier and Customer Representatives and the Approving Committee in detail.

IV.   STS PROGRAM REPRESENTATIVES

The STS Program Representatives are the intermediaries between the supplier and the customer and will be the designated technical contacts for each other for the Ship-to-Stock Program. They will work closely together after approval to ensure that the program is running smoothly during the maintenance phase. One Customer Representative, normally from the quality department, should be assigned for each approved supplier, or group of suppliers, so that the supplier will know whom to contact with any technical questions or concerns. Of course, contractual matters are handled through the Purchasing department.

Customer Representative Responsibilities

Often, the Customer Representative will be the vendor quality engineer, or the inspection supervisor in smaller companies, who first recommends the supplier to the approving committee. The vendor quality engineer is usually the one who is most qualified to judge the acceptability of the product and the supplier's ability to maintain conformance, and the person who would first recognize that the supplier would be a good candidate for the program. There are several main tasks for which the Customer Representative is responsible:

1. The most important responsibility is acting as the liaison between the customer and the supplier. The Customer Representative will be, in many ways, the person who either makes or breaks the program. All questions and problems that the vendor has will be funneled through the Customer Representative (with the exception of purchasing questions) who will be responsible for finding the answers or correcting the problems.

2. The Customer Representative is usually a member of the supplier survey team when the initial surveys are performed.

3. One of the forms required by the Ship-to-Stock Program is the Characteristic Accountability Report. This form is initiated by the Customer Representative and completed by the supplier. The Customer Representative will then verify the report during the qualification process and subsequent audits. The Characteristic Accountability Report is described in Section VI. Product Qualification.

4. The Customer Representative will monitor the consecutive lot by lot inspections to ensure that the correct quality levels are met during qualification.

5. If, at any time, problems arise, the Customer Representative will be responsible for initiating and monitoring corrective actions.

6. Also during the maintenance phase, the Customer Representative must determine when to perform audits of incoming Ship-to-Stock material and will monitor and report the results of the audits.

Supplier Representative Responsibilities

The Supplier Representative will usually be a quality engineer, or inspection supervisor, who is familiar with the part and its process. The Supplier Representative also has responsibilities to help ensure the success of the program.

1. The Supplier Representative shall perform or oversee an outgoing shipping audit before Ship-to-Stock product leaves the supplier's facility for conformance to all contractual requirements.

2. Each STS shipment must be identified as such by the Supplier Representative, before it leaves the supplier's facility.

3. When the supplier has been approved as a Ship-to-Stock supplier, a log will be maintained by the Supplier Representative that will facilitate tracking of Ship-to-Stock material. This log will be explained in Section IX. Release Procedures.

4. The Supplier Representative will notify the Customer Representative whenever a shipment is ready if the product was source inspected prior to Ship-to-Stock qualification. This notification allows the Customer Representative to source inspect/audit the shipment, if desired.

5. If any problems are found with the shipments, the Supplier Representative must notify the Customer Representative. Between the two of them, most problems can be resolved before the shipment leaves the supplier.

6. The Supplier Representative will also notify the Customer Representative of any changes to the process used to manufacture the qualified part. At the customer's discretion, a requalification may be required to ensure the continued integrity of the Ship-to-Stock Program.

Approving Committee Responsibilities

Many companies use a committee composed of representatives of various departments within the company including Purchasing, Incoming Inspection, Manufacturing, and Quality Engineering. This committee would be responsible to oversee the entire STS Program. If the company has an STS Manager, this person usually chairs the approving committee. By using a committee, all the functions of the company are brought together to buy into and support the program.

The committee will review the initial supplier data usually collected by a Customer Representative who believes that the supplier would make a good candidate for the program. Based on the review, the committee may then accept the supplier as a candidate and proceed with information gathering and the initial meeting. The approving committee may also decide that the supplier is not a good risk and that other suppliers should be pursued first.

After all of the work has been completed (the surveys, inspections, etc.), the approving committee is again asked to review the supplier and grant qualification for the program. While the Customer Representative is responsible for the day to day functioning of his assigned suppliers, the Approving Committee would become involved if major problems arose and corrective action plans or disqualifications become necessary.

V. SUPPLIER SURVEYS

The Ship-to-Stock Program requires that a comprehensive quality survey be performed, in addition to the previously mentioned procurement survey, before the decision is made to approve a supplier. This survey will help the customer decide whether the supplier has a sound quality system and a dependable manufacturing process that will consistently produce quality parts which do not require incoming inspection. This initial survey forms the baseline for system audits performed during the Maintenance Phase of the program.

The system survey examines all of the areas controlling a supplier's product quality to ensure that the supplier's quality system and processes have the necessary elements to produce quality products. The general areas surveyed are:

- Drawing and specification control
- Purchased material control
- Process and product acceptance control
- Material storage, pack and ship, control and record retention
- Quality program management

The system survey is usually conducted by the Customer Representative or an evaluation team. All areas of concern discovered during the survey are discussed with the supplier's management after the survey and resolutions are agreed upon before the report is distributed. Major issues requiring corrective action must be documented and resolved prior to qualification for Ship-to-Stock.

During the system survey, special processes may also be reviewed by the Customer Representative with assistance by process specialists (if required). Amplification of the system survey (checklist) can be found in Appendix C. General guidelines for protocol in conducting a survey can be found in the booklet titled *How to Conduct a Supplier Survey* published by the American Society for Quality Control, Milwaukee, Wisconsin.

If the supplier passes the system survey, the supplier can be further considered as a candidate for the Ship-to-Stock Program by the completion of qualification of each product or product family as described in the next chapter.

VI. PRODUCT QUALIFICATION

After the surveys, each product or product family needs to be qualified on its own merits. Product qualification is based on three criteria:

- Characteristic Accountability Report
- First Article Inspection/Evaluation Test
- Past History, based on Lot-by-Lot Inspections

Characteristic Accountability Report

The Characteristic Accountability Report (Figure 2) is used to document the process(es) used to produce critical or major specification characteristics. Some companies refer to this as the manufacturing quality plan. If the process used by the supplier to manufacture the part is satisfactory, it is frozen for all STS shipments.

The Characteristic Accountability Report is initiated by the Customer Representative (with the assistance of technical experts, as required) who lists all of the necessary quality characteristics for controlled manufacture of the part. The supplier then completes the form by indicating how each characteristic is produced and controlled. Elements to be included on this report are agreed upon during the initial meeting with the supplier and include identifying the following:

- The process or machine producing each listed characteristic
- The points of control for each listed characteristic
- The method and frequency of verification

SHIP-TO-STOCK CHARACTERISTIC ACCOUNTABILITY REPORT

Customer Drawing No.	Rev.	Product Line
Customer Part No.	Rev.	Supplier Name
Supplier Part No.	Rev.	Address
Part Description		

Item	Class	Characteristic* and Tolerance	B/P Loc.	Process/ Machine	Point of Control (In-Process/ Final/Etc.)	Method Measured	Frequency of Insp. (AQL %)

*NOTE: All Critical Product Characteristics must be accounted for.

Remarks:

| Prepared by - Customer | Date | Completed by - Supplier | Date |
| Appr. by - Customer Rep. | Date | Appr. by - Cust. STS Program Mgr. | Date |

Sheet _____ of _____

Figure 2

The Characteristic Accountability Report provides the baseline for process audits performed during the maintenance phase of the Ship-to-Stock Program. Therefore, if the process for a listed characteristic is changed, the supplier must notify the Customer Representative prior to shipping products manufactured with that change. Amplification on the Characteristic Accountability Report and how to complete the form can be found in Appendix E. Some smaller companies who have less formal systems have had the supplier sign off on the customers incoming inspection procedures in lieu of the Characteristic Accountability Report.

First Article Inspection/Evaluation Test

The first article inspection/evaluation test is carried out under the direction of authorized customer personnel. It includes:

- Inspection of every characteristic on the piece or unit inspected
- Evaluation of any special processes used in production
- Evaluation testing (for functional units)

This inspection forms the baseline for product audits performed during maintenance of the program.

Qualification Lot Inspection

The third part of product qualification is the lot-by-lot qualification inspection. For lot-by-lot qualification inspection, the supplier will perform normal outgoing or shipping audits and the customer performs normal incoming or source inspection. Special emphasis is placed on review of critical or major characteristics. Usually, three to five lots are sufficient. The purpose of this series of inspection is to assure process repeatability. Past history is used, at times, to meet this element when the product has a very stable quality history.

VII. SHIP-TO-STOCK BASIC AGREEMENT

In order to effectively implement a Ship-to-Stock Program, an agreement should be signed by the customer procurement management and the supplier's management. This Ship-to-Stock Agreement (Figure 3) should list the terms and conditions of the Ship-to-Stock Program and a brief description of the program requirements. Attached to the agreement should be a supplemental page listing all of the supplier's parts that are qualified for the program. Every purchase order written for a qualified supplier and part should contain a clause referring to the STS agreement.

Like the Characteristic Accountability Report mentioned in Section VI, some companies have had supplier management sign off on the customer's incoming inspection procedures in lieu of the formal Basic Agreement. This can be effective in smaller companies whose systems may be informal. The reader should keep in mind the intent of both the Characteristic Accountability Report and the Basic Agreement which is to attain agreement between Supplier and Customer on manufacturing and inspection requirements. Therefore, the documents can be as simple or as complex as needed for the companies' environments.

SHIP-TO-STOCK SUPPLIER AGREEMENT

Supplier Name and Address

Supplier Code

Ship-to-Stock Agreement No.

PURPOSE
The objective of this document is to define and establish a minimum surveillance and audit program, hereafter referred to as Ship-to-Stock, designed to assure a continuous supply of quality products. This program, if observed and maintained by the supplier, will assure that products shipped under this program will conform to product quality and specification requirements thus enabling the reduction or suspension of normal and routine source or incoming inspection procedures for such products.

SCOPE
The program applies only to those supplier products which successfully pass the product qualification requirements as established below. Those qualified products shall be listed in Appendix A of this document and shall be amended from time to time to reflect the current supplier products qualified for the Ship-to-Stock Program.

PURCHASE AGREEMENT
A. This document is not to be construed as a Purchase Agreement, or in any manner a commitment on the part of the customer to purchase or the supplier to sell any products. The obligations of the customer and the supplier with respect to the actual purchase and sale of products shall be established in any Purchase Agreements separately entered into between the parties.

B. This document in no way limits, supersedes or abrogates any contractual obligation, warranty or other requirement specified in any Purchase Agreement. The supplier shall remain totally responsible for the effective control of product quality and shall ship only products which conform to the requirements of any Purchase Agreement applicable to the products. Implementation of this plan shall not waive the customer's right to perform normal source and incoming inspection procedures and to rightfully reject any product found to be nonconforming pursuant to the requirements of any Purchase Agreement.

PRODUCT QUALIFICATION REQUIREMENTS
Prior to inclusion under the Ship-to-Stock Program, each product must successfully complete a product qualification process consisting of (1) first article inspection, (2) complete characteristic accountability review and (3) a lot by lot inspection of at least three consecutive lots. In addition, ultimate qualification of a product(s) shall be based on the customer's decision that the supplier's tooling and procedures for manufacture, inspection and test of the product(s) are indicative of a quality production process and capable of assuring consistent product quality.

Figure 3 (page 1)

SHIP-TO-STOCK SUPPLIER AGREEMENT

Maintenance Requirements

1. Each product must maintain a delivered quality rating of _____ or higher.

2. Systems audits to be performed_____(Frequency)_____.

3. Process audits to be performed _____(Frequency)_____.

4. Product audits to be performed_____(Frequency)_____.

5. Customer inspection to be performed _____(Frequency)_____.

6. Not more than _____ months may lapse between shipments of qualified products or product families without re-qualification or re-evaluation.

7. Special Requirements:

_____

_____

_____

_____

_____

_____

_____

_____

_____

_____

_____

_____

Figure 3 (page 2)

SHIP-TO-STOCK SUPPLIER AGREEMENT

Authorized Signatures

_____

Supplier CEO or Designee   Date

_____

Supplier STS Representative   Date

_____

Alternate Supplier STS Representative   Date

_____

Customer Procurement Manager   Date

_____

Customer STS Program Manager   Date

_____

Customer STS Representative   Date

Figure 3 (page 3)

SHIP-TO-STOCK SUPPLIER AGREEMENT - ADDENDUM A

Supplier Name _____ Ship-to-Stock Agreement #_____

Qualified Product Listing

Revision _____ Date Issued _____ Superseding Revision _____ Dated _____

Part Name	Description	Date Qualified	Customer Rep.	Comments

Figure 3 (page 4)

VIII.   SHIP-TO-STOCK APPROVAL

When the supplier and product qualification process has been completed, including the signed basic agreement, the documents are presented to the Program Manager or Approving Committee. The STS Approving Committee votes to qualify the supplier/part(s) for the program. If the supplier is granted approval, the STS Program Manager normally presents a letter or certificate of acceptance to the supplier. Figure 4 is a suggested Approval Certificate that may be presented to the supplier upon qualification. Many companies also present a certificate to the Supplier Representative. An example of a Supplier Representative Certificate is shown in Figure 5. It is important to note that this approval should allow a specific supplier facility to ship STS products to *all* customer locations. It is imperative that a customer with multiple sites avoid variations of the STS Program from site to site. Once a supplier is approved, it is approved for *all* customer locations, thereby avoiding overlaps in paperwork and human resources.

(CUSTOMER NAME)

hereby awards this quality certificate to:

_____

entitling you to participate in the

Ship-To-Stock Supplier Quality Program

This certificate attests to evidence of an approved Quality System properly implemented, and
to the integrity of your personnel in respect to the maintenance of high quality standards
in delivered products.
This Certificate shall remain in effect as long as delivery of parts demonstrates the strict
adherence to documented procedures and conformance to all requirements,
specifications and drawings.

Requalification Due   _____

_____   _____
Customer Procurement Manager   Date   STS Program Manager   Date

Figure 4   Example of an Approval Certificate

(CUSTOMER NAME)

Ship-To-Stock Supplier Quality Program
Supplier Representative Certificate

Reposing special trust and confidence in the integrity, diligence, and discretion of

_____

and finding that he has the necessary knowledge, skill, experience,
interest, and impartial judgement to merit special responsibility,

_____ (''Supplier'')

has designated him as its
"Supplier STS Representative"
authorizing him to audit and release qualified conforming
products on its behalf in accordance
with the Ship-to-Stock Supplier Quality Program.

Appointed by: Witnessed by:

_____   _____
(Supplier Name)   STS Program Manager   Date

_____
Authorized Signature   Date

Figure 5   Example of a Supplier Representative Certificate

IX. RELEASE PROCEDURE

Only qualified STS products can be released under this program. All Ship-to-Stock shipments must undergo an outgoing shipping audit performed by the Supplier Representative (or customer authorized alternate). A Product Release Checklist such as Figure 6 should be used unless the supplier has an inspection/audit procedure that meets the intent. This is an important function since experience has shown that it is administrative errors, such as wrong parts or damages, that create extensive problems for the customer.

PRODUCT RELEASE CHECKLIST

The following items must be accounted for by the Supplier Ship-to-Stock Representative for each lot of products. This form is to remain on file at the supplier's facility and made available for review by the customer.

1. Purchase order requirements reviewed and satisfied including part number and revision number(s).   _____

2. Part number completed the qualification process.   _____

3. Part number shipped during the past twelve months.   _____

4. Quality inspection report/route traveler complete and acceptable.   _____

5. Product markings complete and legible.   _____

6. Visual inspection of parts acceptable.   _____

7. Packaging meets specifications.   _____

8. Packing slip stamped, signed and dated.   _____

9. Box containing packing slip stamped or labeled, as required.   _____

10. Completion of special paperwork/requirements, if applicable.   _____

Representative Signature _____

Date _____

Part Number _____

Lot Identification (Packing Slip) Number _____

This form is suggested; a supplier form containing the same information may be used.

Figure 6

After completing the Product Release Checklist, the packing list is stamped with the approval stamp such as Figure 7 and signed by the Customer Representative.

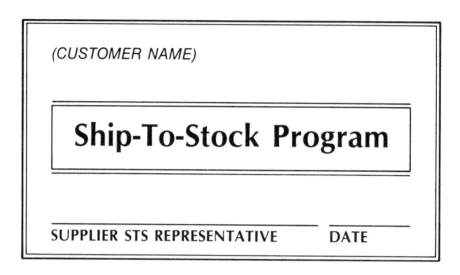

(CUSTOMER NAME)

Ship-To-Stock Program

SUPPLIER STS REPRESENTATIVE   DATE

Figure 7   Ship-to-Stock Stamp and Label

The signature of the Supplier Representative on the stamped packing list attests that the products were manufactured and controlled in conformance with the purchase order and the STS Agreement and that all appropriate inspections were performed as verified by the Supplier Representative during the shipping inspection/audit. It remains obvious that evidence of conformance must be available for review at the supplier's facility.

The Supplier Representative may also identify the outer shipping containers as STS material as specified in the STS Agreement. Often, this is done by placing a sticker or label (or stamping the box) with the release stamp in the area near the packing slip envelope. Be cautioned, this can cause confusion when boxes are recirculated or reused.

If the product being shipped was normally source inspected prior to being qualified for the Ship-to-Stock Program, the Supplier Representative should notify the Customer Representative before shipping the product to allow the customer the option of periodic source inspection or audit.

All Ship-to-Stock shipments must be documented and logged on a form such as Figure 8, which should be available during a customer audit. Again, when the supplier has an equivalent form or report, it should be used thus avoiding the creation of forms extraneous to the supplier's systems and procedures.

It is important for the customer to use the supplier's forms or procedures whenever possible as it would defeat the purpose of the program if every customer implementing STS imposed a new set of forms on the supplier. Of course, the ultimate solution would be a standardization of STS forms throughout industry, therefore minimizing the confusion. This book is intended to assist in the attainment of that goal.

PRODUCT QUALIFICATION AND SHIPPING LOG

Part Number_____ Revision _____

Part Description_____

Characteristic
Accountability _____
                    Date   Performed   Review by   Date

First
Article _____
                    Date   Performed   Review by   Date

Qualification
Completed _____
                    Date   Performed   Review by   Date

STS Lot QTY	Date Shpd	Control No. (Pckg Slp)	Supplier Initials	Remarks
Lot X Lot #1				
Lot X Lot #2				
Lot X Lot #3				
Lot X Lot #4				
Lot X Lot #5				
STS Lot #1				
STS Lot #2				
STS Lot #3				
STS Lot #4				
STS Lot #5				
STS Lot #6				

This form is suggested; a supplier form containing the same information may be used.

Figure 8 (page 1)
(For initial qualification and lot by lot shipments)

PRODUCT QUALIFICATION AND SHIPPING LOG (Continuation Sheet)

Part Number_____ Revision _____

Part Description_____

STS Lot	QTY	Date Shpd	Control No. (Pckg Slp)	Supplier Initials	Remarks

This form is suggested; a supplier form containing the same information may be used.

Figure 8 (page 2)
(For qualified product shipments)

X. MAINTAINING STS STATUS

The terms of the STS Agreement must be maintained to continue shipping qualified parts under the program. This means that:

- The time limit between shipments of the specified part or product family has not been exceeded.
- The manufacturing process of the qualified part does not deviate from the process documented on the Characteristics Accountability Report.
- Any technical problems have been resolved.
- The performance and documentation of shipping audits for STS shipments have been accurately and completely maintained.
- The supplier continues to receive an acceptable quality rating based on the results of periodic inspections and audits.
- No major problems are discovered during auditing which requires suspension of the product from the program until corrective action and corrective action to cause have been accomplished.

If the terms have not been maintained, the Supplier and Customer Representatives should meet to discuss the areas of concern and to implement and monitor a corrective action plan. Auditing is the primary indication of the stability of a supplier's manufacturing and quality system. Experience has shown that this is also true in auditing for compliance to the Ship-to-Stock Program. The following briefly outlines auditing used in the Ship-to-Stock Program.

STS Audits

The Customer Representative should request periodic audits of the supplier's system, process and product to ensure the integrity of the STS program. As with any audit, the supplier should be given reasonable notice before each audit. Alternatives to auditing, such as correlation analysis, may be used. Amplification of the audits discussed below can be found in Appendix D.

System Audits

The Customer Representative should perform system audits, usually annually, to ensure that the supplier's quality system meets the criteria established in the system survey. If the supplier's quality system has deteriorated, the Customer Representative must require corrective action. The Supplier and Customer Representatives should agree on an improvement plan.

Process Audits

The Customer Representative should periodically perform process audits to ensure adherence to the process documented by the Characteristic Accountability Report.

Product Audits

The Customer Representative is responsible for monitoring and evaluating product audits which are based on and compared to the first article inspection. If the audit is performed at the supplier's facility, the supplier's inspectors may be given the responsibility to perform the audit with the Customer Representative verifying the results.

The above audits are not considered to be all-encompassing nor do they release the supplier from his responsibility to have an effective self-audit program. When a supplier has an effective internal audit program, the Customer Representative/auditor can utilize these data to make the Ship-to-Stock maintenance audits more effective.

Periodic Source/Incoming Inspection

Some customers also perform occasional lot inspections as specified in the STS Agreement. These inspections, either source or incoming, are performed to ensure conformance to the STS Agreement. They may be performed in the same manner as qualification lot inspections and their frequency should be specified in the STS Agreement. Examples of such frequencies are one lot per time period, one lot per number of lots or pieces produced, or based on a skip-lot inspection plan. The author believes that this should diminish or be eliminated as the program with the supplier matures; however, this is optional.

XI. STATISTICAL QUALITY CONTROL

When the Ship-to-Stock concept was in its infancy, statistical quality control or process control was not widely used. In fact, statistical process control was generally considered applicable or economically feasible only if you had large volume production. Even with the recent attention to statistical process control brought about by Dr. W. Edwards Deming, many small to medium suppliers have not yet begun to grasp its uses. As a result, the author developed the early Ship-to-Stock Programs around the theory that a total, in-control quality program, verified by auditing, would be as sound as financial or accounting systems which were also verified by auditing. I believe that a customer can establish a Ship-to-Stock Program with a supplier based on auditing.

Some companies have developed their Ship-to-Stock Program solely on the supplier being in statistical control for critical and major product parameters. The author is in favor of statistical process control and feels, if applied properly, it can be an excellent tool to guarantee product quality. Unfortunately, the author has seen many unsophisticated suppliers forced into implementing statistical process control and adopting the extra paperwork without fully understanding its uses. Because so many customers relied heavily on statistical control to assure product quality, the supplier was forced to make control charts and *include them in every shipment*. After the first few shipments, the charts were no longer used by the customer and usually just filed away. In requiring control charts with every shipment, the customer implies that, even though the supplier is a "favored" supplier, the customer does not really trust the supplier and requires statistical data, inspection records and certificates attesting to conformance to continue Ship-to-Stock. All of this, in spite of the excellent product quality history and sound quality management system that made the supplier a Ship-to-Stock candidate in the first place.

Another overplayed misuse of statistics is when the customer's statistician teaches statistical applications for production processes to nearly everyone employed by the supplier in "just one or two days." Who is kidding whom? If the supplier understands statistical quality control, then the supplier's personnel probably understand it as well. But if the suppliers do not want to jeopardize any future business, they will probably agree to classes and thank the customer's management for the new information.

Statistics can play an important part in Ship-to-Stock but it must be integrated into the whole quality system. No one can become a statistician or can be taught to think statistically in a few easy lessons. Effective applications of statistics take a lot of learning to be properly applied at the right time. Statistical charts for the sake of accepting shipments lend no real value to the process and are a waste of money.

XII.   ELECTRONIC COMPONENTS: SHIP-TO-STOCK

Experience has shown that the Characteristic Accountability Report does not lend itself to the manufacture of electrical components. In the component world, the performance to electronic function is the critical issue. Here the list of parameters is extensive and several phases of the process may relate to one parameter. It has been found that aligning the specification between the customer and the supplier, coupled with inspection and test correlation, is more effective than using the Characteristic Accountability Report. To use the Ship-to-Stock Program for electrical components, products are selected by family or manufacturing groups based on product history. The customer must then align his purchase specification with the supplier's data book parameters. The next step is to begin correlation analysis between the customer and the supplier until the test programs are also aligned. If the defective parts per million (ppm) quantity is at an acceptable level, and if the test programs are aligned, Ship-to-Stock can begin.

Some major customers extend the qualification procedure to include supplier quality system review, electrical certification, visual/mechanical certifications and manufacturing process certification. Once the above is certified and agreed upon, the process flow is approved and frozen and any changes to the process require customer notification. Like Ship-to-Stock with other commodities, periodic auditing or re-evaluation of the product is performed. Systems and processes may be audited at the supplier's facility to verify the stability of the agreed upon, and previously documented, process. This can be unmanageable when processing is spread throughout the world and some calculated risk-taking may be required. Also, since components often look alike, it may be advantageous for the customer to perform a visual incoming inspection of each lot to ensure that no administrative errors have been made.

An amplified example of this method is found in the American Society for Quality Control, Annual Quality Congress Transactions 1985 "QuEST, Quality Enhanced Supplier Test" by Raymond Pelchat, p. 41.

With the increase in surface mount technology in the component world, a customer may find that the cost of automated test equipment required to handle large volumes of these devices is astronomical. For Ship-to-Stock, the correlation of test and product history review can be pushed back into the supplier's facility. In this case, the customer reviews the supplier's lot by lot test methodology and the supplier's in-house product yields and, if the parts per million/billion (PPM/PPB) is at a tolerable rate, the process is frozen and Ship-to-Stock is begun. Obviously, any life testing or qualification test history is also analyzed.

One closer working relationship is when the customer has production failure monitoring. For example, with respect to electronic components, some customers have developed computerized board level failure monitoring. The computer usually selects components which are probable causes for board failures and then these "failures" are verified for each supplier. These verified board level failures are then fed back to the supplier in the form of a trend report. This approach can reduce or eliminate other forms of verification, such as product audits and periodic incoming inspection.

Field failure monitoring, which is similar to and often combined with the above, is also beginning to be used by some customers in lieu of auditing.

This is the ultimate of the Ship-to-Stock philosophy with a true close working relationship between the customer and the supplier. One will also note that this is Ship-to-Stock with no redundant expense for incoming inspection. At least three major U.S. manufacturers are using this philosophy at the time of this writing.

XIII.   IMPORTANCE OF THE PARTNERSHIP CONCEPT

You have probably noticed by now that the Ship-to-Stock program requires a close working relationship between the customer and the supplier. This relationship can only be established with commitment and communication between both parties from the representatives through top management. At the beginning, the program also requires time and money; however, both are more than paid back as more, and better quality, products are qualified for the program.

The representatives cannot be allowed to work in a vacuum. They must be allowed to audit and communicate with their suppliers during the good times — not just when problems occur. Auditing during the good times provides both parties the opportunity to prevent problems in a clear atmosphere; whereas a supplier visit on a "fire fighting" mission only serves to narrow the scope of communication and cloud the issues.

A Ship-to-Stock program will also weaken if qualified products are forgotten. Ship-to-Stock cannot work if the customer skimps on audits or restricts travel to the supplier. Hence, top management must allot the time and budget to communicate effectively. Without top management commitment, failure is inevitable.

Top management should also focus on the long range. A customer may not be able to forecast specific long range requirements, but surely long term agreements can, and should, be made with their key, that is, their Ship-to-Stock suppliers. By taking the time and spending the effort required to qualify a supplier, it is foolish not to expect (and receive) top quality parts from the STS-qualified supplier for the life of the part or product. The longer the supplier is expected to supply the part, the more committed he will be to supply you with acceptable parts as requirements or specifications change. He will also come to know your needs and manufacturing requirements and will be more willing to be flexible as specifications and requirements change. As a result, your success becomes the supplier's success.

Always keep in mind that STS parts may *initially* cost a little more than parts procured from other suppliers. However, consider the possibility of paying a few pennies less per part only to constantly 100 percent inspect, disposition and return all of the parts that do not meet specifications. Consider too the problems created for your manufacturing lines as nonconforming parts are found that were missed during incoming inspection. Then consider what it will be like to only deal with suppliers with whom you are constantly in touch, whose ability to produce quality parts is proven and whom you never need to inspect, just audit. It only makes sense to choose your suppliers carefully, state your requirements specifically and audit parts on a regular basis. Ship-to-Stock is more than just a commitment to a quality program, it is a commitment to a quality partnership.

XIV.   SUPPLIER RECOGNITION

From both the supplier's and the customer's viewpoints, Ship-to-Stock is an honors program. Rewards should be given for this accomplishment.

In most companies, a suitable plaque is awarded to the supplier for display in the supplier lobby. To a visitor, it is an impressive sight to see numerous awards displayed in the lobby of the supplier.

Some companies have held large banquets at the customer's corporate office to award the plaque to one or two of the supplier's management. In my opinion, the award should be presented to the supplier's management on the shop floor with the work force present. After all, the work force made the good products that are shipped to stock. Also there should be some small token (such as a key chain) for each supplier employee. Do not forget the Supplier Representative who performed the shipping audits. Give him or her a plaque or at least a framed certificate.

Above all, recognize your good suppliers at the inception of the program and on each anniversary.

XV.   SHIP-TO-STOCK AND JUST-IN-TIME

Just-in-Time (JIT) is a concept that can be broken up into two segments: JIT procurement and JIT inventory. Just-in-Time procurement involves scheduling and receiving purchased goods in such a manner that the customer carries almost no purchased goods inventory.

Just-in-Time inventory relates to work-in-process inventory at a near zero level and does not relate to Ship-to-Stock.

Ship-to-Stock is a program that focuses on the reduction of material acquisition costs related to the quality function. Ship-to-Stock operates under the premise than an *effective* total quality control system yields products that fit the customer's needs. As the previous chapters have shown, Ship-to-Stock qualifies a product by verifying the design and the process which makes the product and then emphasizes auditing and periodic inspections to verify that the process does not change.

Ship-to-Stock further emphasizes that the cost of qualification and preventative audits is less costly than the traditional methods of after-the-fact appraisal inspection.

Just-in-Time procurement focuses on the above but also includes such additional elements of rigid forecasting and scheduling, inventory carrying costs, traffic and transportation costs, etc.

In conclusion, one can see Ship-to-Stock as a forerunner to JIT procurement. With Ship-to-Stock in place, the company can then focus on the many additional issues involving Just-in-Time.

3

Definitions

Inspection — The process of measuring, examining, testing, gauging or otherwise comparing the unit with the applicable requirements.[1]

100% Inspection — The inspection of all parts in a lot for all characteristics to ensure compliance to specifications.

Acceptance Sampling — Sampling inspection in which decisions are made to accept or not accept product or service; the methodology that deals with procedures by which decisions to accept or not accept are based on the results of the inspection of samples.[2]

Skip-Lot — In acceptance sampling, a plan in which some lots in a series are accepted without inspection when the sampling results for a stated number of immediately preceding lots meet stated criteria.[3]

Incoming Inspection — The inspection of purchased parts at the customer's facility after the shipment of parts from the supplier to ensure supplier compliance with specifications and contractual agreements.

Source Inspection — The inspection of purchased parts at the supplier's facility by a Customer Representative to ensure supplier compliance with specifications and contractual agreements.

- - - - - - - - - - - - - - - - - - - -

1 *American National Standard: Terms, Symbols and Definitions for Acceptance Sampling*, American Society for Quality Control, Milwaukee, Wis., 1978, p. 3
2 Ibid, p. 1.
3 Ibid, p. 10.

Ship-to-Stock	— A program in which the supplier and customer work together for improved quality and conformance of manufactured parts to eliminate the need for incoming or source inspection of purchased parts or products. Under this program, individual products or processes are qualified as opposed to an overall supplier certification. Also, maintenance of this program is provided through audits.
Survey	— Broad overview of a supplier's system or process used to evaluate the adequacy of that system or process to produce quality products.
System Survey	— A survey conducted to assess whether the supplier has appropriately controlled systems which will adequately prevent the manufacture of nonconforming products.
Process Survey	— A survey used to evaluate whether a supplier has process controls in place to ensure that the supplier's process will manufacture quality products. Process controls include proper tooling, equipment, inspection, etc.
Audits	— A systematic examination of the acts and decisions with respect to quality in order to independently verify or evaluate compliance to the operational requirements of the quality program or the specifications or contract requirements of the product or service.[4] Audits of a supplier's quality system or process must be performed at the supplier's facility. Audits of a supplier's product may be performed either at the supplier's facility or in-house.
System Audit	— A documented activity performed to verify, by examination and evaluation of objective evidence, that applicable elements of the quality system are suitable and have been developed, documented and effectively implemented in accordance with specified requirements.[5]
Process Audit	— An analysis of elements of a process and appraisal of completeness, correctness or conditions and probable effectiveness.[6]
Product Audit	— A quantitative assessment of conformance to required product characteristics.[7]
Supplier Certification	— A program aimed at qualifying suppliers already on an approved status to a higher level of approval called certification. This usually encompasses review of the supplier's past delivered product history, and an indepth quality system survey. Certification of a supplier is usually all encompassing covering all products. Once certification is granted to a supplier, the customer institutes a reduced sampling at incoming inspection.

- - - - - - - - - - - - - - - - - -

4 *American National Standard: Quality Systems Terminology*, American Society for Quality Control, Milwaukee, Wis., 1978, p. 5.

5 *American National Standard: Quality Systems Terminology*, American Society for Quality Control, Milwaukee, Wis., 1978, p. 5.

6 Ibid, p. 6.

7 Ibid, p. 6.

4

Appendices

MANAGEMENT INFORMATION SYSTEMS IN SUPPORT OF SHIP-TO-STOCK

The basic information needed to support a Ship-to-Stock Program is a supplier rating system. Supplier rating systems run the gamut from simple manual systems to complex computer systems. At one end of the spectrum, your system may be limited to a simple lot rating index dividing the number of lots accepted by the number of lots received.

$$\text{Rating} = \frac{\text{Number of lots accepted}}{\text{Number of lots received}}$$

When this is done for each part number received, a review of the ratings should lead you toward suppliers and/or part numbers that should first be considered for a Ship-to-Stock Program.

A more advanced rating system might have several ratings, including a Quality System Rating and a Product Rating. A Quality System Rating, based on the supplier survey, would result in the supplier being placed in one of three categories:

- *Approved status*, indicating that the supplier has an effective quality system in place.
- *Conditional approval status*, indicating that the supplier's system has minor deficiencies and that a corrective action plan is in place. Conditional approval status may change to approved status when corrective actions are verified by the customer engineer.
- *Not approved status*, indicating that the supplier cannot become approved without major improvements to the quality system.

The Product Rating is comprised of one or more of the following:

$$\text{Lot Rating} = \frac{\text{Number of lots accepted}}{\text{Number of lots received}} \times 100$$

$$\text{Part Rating} = \frac{\text{\# of pieces accepted in the sample}}{\text{\# of pieces in the inspection sample}} \times 100$$

$$\text{Delivery Rating} = \frac{\text{Number of days early (or late)}}{\text{Demerit + Completeness factor}} \times 100$$

These ratings can be combined to represent a composite Product Rating for all lots received for a particular product or product family and then combined into the supplier's overall rating.

With this information in a computer data base, the data can easily be sorted and manipulated based on specific parameters to yield information which can be used as a basis to direct labor for the best dollar return.

Some examples are:

- All lots with a percent rating of XX to YY.
- Minimum number of lots received.
- Minimum number of pieces received.
- Supplier XYZ.

For examples of Ship-to-Stock potential reports, see Figures 9, 10 and 11.

This information enables the customer engineer to focus on products that are high quality and high volume to attain the largest return on the investment.

A more complex information system might also collect incoming inspection labor hours for each lot inspected and sort the information in a labor hours Pareto analysis. By analyzing these data with the supplier ratings and sorting the information, you will be able to identify the high quality/high volume products that consume the most incoming inspection time. You will probably learn that the 80-20 principle applies to inspection times, that is, 80 percent of your inspection time is consumed by 20 percent of your products.

The Pareto analysis by labor hours not only identifies the good products that consume inspection time, but also identifies the poor products that require extensive inspection time which need corrective action.

If this information cannot be easily added to the rating system, it can be approximated by direct contact with the incoming manager who will be glad to tell you which parts require excess time and which ones are always brief.

In an even more sophisticated computer system, you can have the system automatically flag for Ship-to-Stock Product audit requirements. These audit flags may be based on time (one lot per month or quarter) or number of pieces (one product for every 50,000 pieces received). In a multiplant company, it is very helpful for the system to be linked between plants. If the system is linked between plants, the product audit requirement can be flagged regardless of the receiving location. One major computer manufacturer is interlinked via tele-networking so that monitoring of the Ship-to-Stock Program is worldwide and real-time.

Remember that the product audit can be conducted in two ways. It can be performed in the supplier's facility by the Supplier Representative, and reviewed by the Customer Representative, or the audit can be performed by the Customer Representative in the customer's incoming inspection area. The audit flags must be set so that ample time is allowed for the Customer Representative to arrange for the audit to be performed at either location. If the audit requirement information is printed in a report format, it can also be used to report delinquent audits.

The final addition to your computer system is tracking of cost savings and cost avoidances. Since few of us have the luxury of a complete cost of quality tracking system, an alternative approach to reporting savings is to code each lot received as an inspection lot or a Ship-to-Stock lot. With this information, you can take the total number of lots inspected for a specific period and divide this into the incoming inspection budget for that same period. This yields the average cost per lot inspected. This cost multiplied by the number of lots that are shipped to stock yields the cost savings. The author considers this one of the prime uses of a computer tracking system as all manufacturing is measured (and all bonuses given) based on a job well done that has been measured in dollars.

It has been the author's intent to outline the areas in which a management information system can be a useful tool in implementing and monitoring a Ship-to-Stock Program. Specific details of each area could each fill a book; hence, they are left to the reader to expand on and implement in his information system regardless of how large or how small that system is. Unfortunately there is no canned package that meets the requirements for all companies for supplier ratings and cost of quality tracking. Each system must be tailored to fit the individual needs of each company.

```
REPORT NO. STS001                                                          PAGE: 1
RUN DATE: 11/06/84                                    DATE RANGE: 10/84 TO 10/84

                         SUPPLIER QUALITY RATING SYSTEM
                     SHIP-TO-STOCK POTENTIAL CANDIDATE REPORT
                                       BY
                          PART NO, SUPPLIER, AREA CODE

        PART (Family or No.): A00    RATING: 99% - 100%    MIN LOTS: 5    MIN PIECES: 10000

                                              AREA      LOTS       PIECES
      PART NUMBER    SUPPLIER CODE    SUPPLIER NAME    CODE    RECEIVED    RECEIVED    RATING
      ===========    =============    =============    ====    ========    ========    ====

      A00 - 1234     A5600 - 04          ABC CO.         A        7        134,654    100.00%
                                                              --------    --------    ----
                                  * Part Number Subtotal:        7        134,654    100.00%

      A00 - 1235     X2500 - 01          XYZ CO.         B        6         21,000    100.00%
                                                              --------    --------    ----
                                  * Part Number Subtotal:        6         21,000    100.00%

                                                              ========    ========    ====
                              ** A00 PART FAMILY TOTAL:         13        155,654    100.00%
```

NOTE: The STS Part Number Report sorts by part number series, supplier and inspection area
        with parameters set at (for Figure 9):
          • Rating: 99-100%
          • Minimum number of lots: 5 per period
          • Minimum number of pieces: 10,000

Figure 9   STS Part Number Report

```
REPORT NO. STS002                                                                    PAGE: 1
RUN DATE: 11/06/84                                              DATE RANGE: 10/84 TO 10/84

                              SUPPLIER QUALITY RATING SYSTEM
                        SHIP-TO-STOCK POTENTIAL CANDIDATE REPORT
                                            BY
                            AREA CODE, PART NUMBER, SUPPLIER

                AREA CODE: A    RATING: 99% - 100%    MIN LOTS: 5    MIN PIECES: 10000

  AREA                                                  LOTS       PIECES
  CODE   PART NUMBER   SUPPLIER CODE   SUPPLIER NAME   RECEIVED   RECEIVED   RATING
  ===    =========     ==========      ==========      ======     ======     ====

   A     A00 - 0009    A5600 - 04      ABC CO.            6         12,573    100.00%

   —     A00 - 1036    A5600 - 04      ABC CO.            7         61,000    100.00%

   —     A00 - 3054    X2500 - 01      XYZ CO.           12         16,500    100.00%

   —     A00 - 3055    X2500 - 01      XYZ CO.           13         16,100    100.00%
                                                       ------      ------     ----
                                    * A00 FAMILY TOTAL:   38        106,173   100.00%

   A     A01 - 0113    A5600 - 04      ABC CO.            6         36,000    100.00%
                                                       ------      ------     ----
                                    * A01 FAMILY TOTAL:    6         36,000   100.00%

                                                       ======      ======     ====
                                    ** A AREA TOTAL:      44        142,173   100.00%
```

NOTE: The STS Inspection Area Report sorts by inspection area, part number and supplier with
        parameters set at (for Figure 10):
        • Rating: 99-100%
        • Minimum number of lots: 5 per period
        • Minimum number of pieces: 10,000

Figure 10   STS Inspection Area Report

```
REPORT NO. STS003                                                          PAGE:  1
RUN DATE: 11/06/84                                    DATE RANGE: 05/84 TO 11/84

                        SUPPLIER QUALITY RATING SYSTEM
                   SHIP-TO-STOCK POTENTIAL CANDIDATE REPORT
                                      BY
                       SUPPLIER, PART NO. AREA CODE

        SUPPLIER CODE: A5600 - 04    RATING: 95% - 100%    MIN LOTS: 4    MIN PIECES: 0

                                             AREA     LOTS      PIECES
     SUPPLIER CODE   SUPPLIER NAME   PART NUMBER  CODE   RECEIVED  RECEIVED   RATING
     =============   =============   ==========   ===    ========  ========   ====

     A5600 - 04      ABC CO.         A00 - 1100     A        4       2,594    100.00%
         —               —           A00 - 1100     B        7       7,286    100.00%

         —               —           A00 - 1118     A        5       7,754    100.00%
                                                          --------  --------   ----
                          * A00 PART FAMILY SUBTOTAL:      16      17,634    100.00%


     A5600 - 04      ABC CO.         A01 - 3071     C        6         357    100.00%
                                                          --------  --------   ----
                          * A01 PART FAMILY SUBTOTAL:       6         357    100.00%


                                                          ========  ========   ====
                        ** A5600-04 SUPPLIER TOTAL:        22      17,991    100.00%
```

NOTE: The STS Supplier Report sorts by supplier, part number and inspection area with
        parameters set at (for Figure 11):
        • Rating: 99-100%
        • Minimum number of lots: 4 per period
        • Minimum number of pieces: 0

Figure 11   STS Supplier Report

APPENDIX B

ECONOMIC ANALYSIS AND PROGRAM DEVELOPMENT

An effective Ship-to-Stock Program involves quality planning, including process controls and audits, and can offer equal or better quality protection than traditional source and incoming inspection methods. The question arises, "What are the cost savings of a Ship-to-Stock Program?" Figuring the cost savings of a Ship-to-Stock Program can be easy with a few assumptions and calculations.

Start with the premise that incoming inspections are responsible for the majority of purchased material quality costs. Then assume that the Ship-to-Stock quality cost is derived from the qualification of specific items plus traveling and auditing expenses. The general savings model of an established Ship-to-Stock Program can be stated as follows:

$$C_I + Q - C_A = \text{Ship-to-Stock Savings.}$$

Where C_I = incoming inspection costs *not* incurred as a result of bypassing incoming inspection.

Q = improved quality and reliability as a result of early quality planning.

C_A = cost of audits, including product qualification and travel.

Calculating Incoming Inspection Costs (C_I)

To determine the cost of incoming inspection, the following formula can be used:

$$C_I = L + I + S + R + E + C$$

Where L = inspection labor.

I = interest (while product is in inspection area).

S = incoming inspection space (where product is held for inspection).

R = handling of all rejects.

E = quality engineering and planning related to incoming inspection.

C = capital equipment usage.

The key factor in incoming inspection costs is labor expended to appraise the quality of incoming lots. Labor actually makes up 70 to 80 percent of the cost savings.

Calculating Improved Quality and Reliability (Q)

Without sufficient historical data, a quantitative value on the improvement in quality (Q) cannot be set. It can be assumed that early planning, or prevention costs, yields a 5-to-1 return on appraisal costs due to the greater care taken to assure that each product has the necessary controls in place before it is qualified for Ship-to-Stock. In the following calculations, however, the author will consider the savings from improved quality to be zero (0).

Calculating Auditing Costs (C_A)

The cost of audits (C_A) and monitoring the program is prorated based on the number of workdays used by a Customer Representative to perform all of the audits needed to monitor the program. (Usually, the program can be maintained effectively with one to two days per quarter to perform audits at the supplier's facility and one day of in-house monitoring.)

Potential Ship-to-Stock Savings

TOTAL AVOIDED   TOTAL COST
INCOMING INSPECTION — TO MONITOR = $$ SAVED
OF SELECTED PARTS   PROGRAM

$$C_I - C_A \qquad = \$\$ \text{ SAVED}$$

The summation of avoided incoming inspection costs (C_I) for all products purchased from one qualified supplier, minus the total cost of auditing (C_A), that supplier yields the annual potential savings. In one example, shipping one product (a complex machined casting for a disk drive) to stock yielded the following savings. Each piece took 45 minutes to inspect.

$$
\begin{aligned}
&\quad \$8,702.16\ (C_I) \\
+ &\quad\quad 0.00\ (Q) \\
- &\quad 2,325.00\ (C_A) \\
\hline
= &\quad \$6,377.16\ \text{(or Ship-to-Stock savings)}
\end{aligned}
$$

General Considerations

Ship-to-Stock Program costs include expenses for program development, supplier qualification and program maintenance. Some of these may or may not be included in the general savings model depending on the particular company's accounting policies since some costs, especially development costs, are considered one-time expenditures.

Program Maintenance Costs

Program maintenance costs would include the following:

• Audits, which include system, process and product.
• Periodic source or incoming inspections.
• General overhead or administrative costs.

Breakeven Point

Often, you can use a breakeven point to determine potential cost savings or to determine which suppliers to begin working with on the program. In one company, the breakeven point is 10 inspection labor hours per month. If a supplier's product requires more than 10 inspection hours per month and is within a 300-mile radius of a plant or regional auditor, they can audit with less expense than with incoming inspection. Keep in mind that they are dealing with only top-quality suppliers. If the supplier is more distant or the nature of the product is such that auditing is required more often than on a monthly basis, the breakeven point per supplier is slightly higher. On the other hand, if more than one supplier can be audited during a trip or the product complexity is simple (e.g., die controlled), the audits are less frequent and the breakeven point is lowered. Furthermore, once a supplier is qualified for Ship-to-Stock, the incremental costs to place additional products into the plan encompass primarily the cost of qualification as there is relatively little incremental cost associated with auditing. With regular inspection, however, the more one procures the more one spends on inspection. This is illustrated in the following figure.

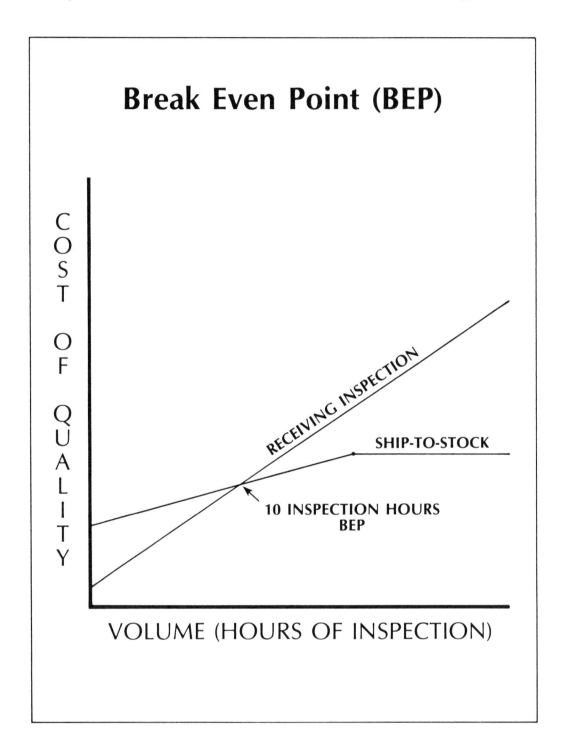

Figure 12

40

Dollar Volume

Often products that require extensive incoming inspection due to tight tolerances or geometric complexity, or products received in volume, make up the majority of material acquisition costs. As a consequence, by shipping these products to stock, you can account for as much as 50 percent of the total acquisition dollars by having only 10 to 15 percent of the supplier base on the program. Also, this is a good leverage tool to encourage the purchasing department to place new products, which are likely Ship-to-Stock candidates, with the better suppliers or with suppliers that are already involved in a similar program.

Immediate and Long-Term Potentials

For starters, by taking all products requiring more than the breakeven point of 10 inspection hours, and subtracting the poor quality products and suppliers, one can define the total immediate potential. Also, by identifying products with a poor quality history, and solving these problems using the Pareto principle, you can place more products on the program in order to yield additional long-term savings. In this way, the immediate potential, plus an estimated percentage of the long-term potential, becomes the *actual* savings potential, and in a large company, the corporate-wide savings can be in the hundreds of thousands of dollars. In two multidivisional companies with sales in the $2 billion area, documented savings have been over $1 million in the first year of full implementation of the program with upwards to $10 million in later years. This is impressive but one must remember that proportional savings are available to the smaller companies. One small company producing grandfather clocks with slightly over 100 employees implemented a program in five months. By reducing the number of pendulum suppliers from three to one and eliminating an operation, the net result was a savings of $50,000. Additional examples of cost savings are shown in Figure 13.

Development and Implementation

Program Development

Experience shows that the cost of one qualified Supplier Engineer for a period of one and one-half years should be allotted for the development of a corporate program. The tasks would include:

- Defining the initial philosophy.
- Establishing qualification criteria for both supplier and products.
- Setting up and administering pilot programs with two suppliers.
- Establishing economic models and forecasting methods.
- Writing "how to" guide books and other documentation for program personnel.
- Training and consulting with plant personnel until they are self-sufficient in the program.

Supplier Implementation

Supplier implementation costs will vary depending on the supplier and the part being considered. It is recommended that you start with a supplier who has consistent high quality or a supplier who is on a similar program with another company.

Supplier costs would include:

- Supplier selection
- Presentation of program to supplier and supplier survey
- Review of requirements and release documents with the supplier
- Establishing specific audit criteria
- Initial orientation and auditing by the Customer Representative.

SOME ACTUAL EXAMPLES
OF
ANNUAL SAVINGS ARE:

$6K/Part Number

$23K/Supplier

$200K/Plant

$1-10 Million/Corporation

Figure 13

APPENDIX C

SUPPLIER QUALITY SYSTEM AND
PROCUREMENT SURVEY CHECKLISTS

Supplier Quality System Survey Checklist

This appendix will help define the type of quality system survey that should be performed by the Customer Representative in order to support the Ship-to-Stock Program.

A complete system *survey* should be performed as part of the initial qualification procedure. A complete system *audit*, based on the initial survey, should be performed annually by the Customer Representative (refer to Appendix D). This may be performed during one visit or several visits throughout the year.

A summary report of the survey should be completed and copies supplied to the Program Manager. The Customer Representative must review the survey results with the supplier management and ensure that corrective actions are implemented as necessary.

Principles of a Quality Survey

a. It is a basic premise that surveys are to be conducted in a professional manner and nonconformances be handled immediately in a constructive manner.

b. Success in performing effective surveys requires a thorough knowledge of quality principles by the evaluator.

c. The survey cannot be performed in the Quality Manager's office or in a conference room.

d. The evaluator should maintain control of the survey and not be led by the supplier.

e. You must survey "where the action is" on the production floor.

f. Verify all verbal information.

g. *Prepare* for each survey by establishing checklists that are appropriate for the supplier and product.

h. Modify checklists for each supplier to ensure the most effective survey.

i. Discuss findings informally before the closing conference to be sure of all of your facts.

j. Top management must be involved in the closing conference when the program needs their attention.

k. Follow up on survey areas needing corrective action or the whole effort will be a waste of time.

l. The survey is to ensure that the supplier has established an adequate quality system.

m. Above all, be realistic, firm and fair.

Ship-to-Stock Survey Plan

The Customer Representative must establish a plan that includes all phases of the supplier's system. The attached survey can be used for all initial STS qualifying surveys and the annual audits. This survey may be used in whole or in part as applicable to the complexity of the supplier's quality systems and the products manufactured.

The survey format should not be considered to be complete and unchangeable. It should be used as a basic guideline to establish a survey plan that properly meets the needs of product requirements; and also, is specific enough in detail to apply to the systems and processes of the particular supplier under Ship-to-Stock agreement.

The survey contains six general categories which are valued at 100 points. Each question in a category is to be answered and given a point value of 0 to 100. Keep in mind that the supplier system is being evaluated on the system's ability to yield product that will not need customer incoming inspection. The summation of the point values divided by the number of questions will give the category point average. If a question does not apply to the supplier, mark the question N/A (not applicable) and do not include the question in the category point average.

The final score is the summation of the categories' point averages divided by the number of categories used.

In assigning point values, keep in mind the following guidelines:

100 points = excellent (this is an attainable score)
 75 points = commercial average
 50 points = unacceptable

The author has found that if the STS evaluator and the supplier's quality person each answer questions fairly and assign point values independently during the survey, both will be amazed at the similarity of the point values given when the final scores are tabulated. The author further promotes that the following scale be used because we all recognize the scores of:

90 - 100 = A or excellent - approved
80 - 89 = B or good - approved
70 - 79 = C or average - conditional approval
60 - 69 = D or poor - disapproved
50 - 59 = F or failure - disapproved

Index
Ship-To-Stock System Survey

1. Drawing and Specification Control
2. Purchased Material Control
3. Measuring and Testing Equipment Control
4. Process Control and Product Acceptance
5. Material Storage Area, Packing, Shipping and Record Retention Control
6. Quality Program Management
7. Strength Summary of System Survey
8. Corrective Action Summary of System Survey
9. Summary Report, Combined Rating

Ship-To-Stock
Supplier Quality System Survey/Audit

Supplier _____

Address _____

City, State _____ Telephone _____

Survey/Audit Completion Date _____

Supplier Quality Manager _____

Category I. Drawing and Specification Control	Yes	No	Point Value
A) Changes are coordinated with customer procurement authority.	____	____	____
B) Drawing change notification system assures that appropriate personnel are receiving documents on current basis.	____	____	____
C) Records on effectivity of changes are maintained.	____	____	____
D) Obsolete drawings and specifications in production and inspection are withdrawn from use.	____	____	____
E) File system assures obsolete drawings and specifications are identified and segregated from current issues.	____	____	____
F) Drawings and specifications with unauthorized markings, notes, etc., are withdrawn from use.	____	____	____
G) Applicable engineering changes and letters are referenced on procedures, inspection and test records, travelers, etc.	____	____	____
H) Systems provide controlled distribution and records of drawings and specifications including revision status.	____	____	____

Category I Point Average (1-100) ____

Category I Notes

_____

_____

_____

_____

_____

_____

_____

_____

_____

_____

Category II. Purchased Material Control	Yes	No	Point Value
A) All required references (drawings and specifications, special process control and inspection/test requirements) are given to the supplier with the PO.	___	___	___
B) Purchase order requirements are available to incoming inspection for adequate checks of certification of conformance/tests received from the supplier.	___	___	___
C) Procedures adhere to designated sampling plans, procedures and AQL limits.	___	___	___
D) Inspectors adhere to designated sampling plans, procedures and AQL limits.	___	___	___
E) Measuring/testing equipment specified and utilized.	___	___	___
F) Raw material is laboratory tested when required by PO; otherwise, certificate of test is applicable.	___	___	___
G) Objective evidence of material and product inspections/tests are documented on appropriate records.	___	___	___
H) Inspection and test status of purchased items and material is effectively indicated.	___	___	___
I) Appropriate segregation is provided for raw, nonconforming, and accepted material, and material pending inspection and/or test.	___	___	___
J) Plan for control of conformance assures effective supplier corrective action.	___	___	___
K) Plan for rating supplier's performance is in operation and utilized for control of purchases.	___	___	___
L) Plan provides for effective control and appraisal of characteristics which cannot be inspected at incoming (for example, nondestructive testing, heat treat, chemical analysis).	___	___	___
M) Plan assures that supplier's special processes (heat treating, brazing, etc.) are currently certified.	___	___	___
N) Current evidence of buyer's approval is maintained when buyer-qualified suppliers are utilized in lieu of supplier inhouse facilities.	___	___	___

Category II Point Average (1-100) ___

Category **II** Notes

_____

_____

_____

_____

_____

_____

_____

_____

_____

_____

Category III. Measuring and Testing Equipment Control	Yes	No	Point Value
A) Equipment calibrated at established intervals.	_____	_____	____
B) Records verify calibration and traceability to national standards.	_____	_____	____
C) Test and measurement equipment calibrated within established intervals.	_____	_____	____
D) Provision for known location in effect to assure availability for periodic calibration.	_____	_____	____
E) Items labeled, tagged, or otherwise identified as required to reflect serviceability date and date of next calibration.	_____	_____	____
F) Calibration records contain information required for controlling scheduling frequency.	_____	_____	____
G) Unqualified equipment identified to show its status and prevent its use.	_____	_____	____
H) Handling practices in storage and at points of use are adequate to ensure accuracy of devices is maintained.	_____	_____	____

Category III Point Average (1-100)   ____

Category III Notes

_____

_____

_____

_____

_____

_____

_____

_____

_____

Category IV. Process Control and Product Acceptance	Yes	No	Point Value
A) Process instructions, procedure sheets, travelers, etc., are utilized and contain requirements of each operation for manufacturing and inspection control.	_____	_____	____
B) Operator's and inspector's identification are applied to operations as required.	_____	_____	____
C) Extent and degree of inspection/test is applied.	_____	_____	____
D) Status of lots and/or items is shown on tags, routing cards, move tickets, totebox cards, etc.	_____	_____	____
E) Appropriate hold, rework and scrap tags or forms are utilized as required.	_____	_____	____
F) Nonconforming items are removed from normal channels and placed in appropriate isolation areas.	_____	_____	____
G) Rework conducted with authorized and documented procedures and subject to inspection/test.	_____	_____	____
H) Corrective action forms and procedures utilized to prevent and/or control recurrence of defects.	_____	_____	____
I) Final inspection and test conducted in conformance with applicable procedures, travelers, plans, etc.	_____	_____	____
J) Final inspection and test conducted to verify completion and acceptance status of characteristics controlled by in-process inspection and test.	_____	_____	____
K) Inspection records are completed and include part and lot control number, customer, engineering changes, lot and sample size, characteristics inspected, quantity accepted and rejected, inspector's identification and inspection date.	_____	_____	____
L) Items and/or lots released for shipping and stores contain evidence of inspection/test performance.	_____	_____	____
M) Personnel and/or equipment certification conducted in conformance with applicable specifications.	_____	_____	____
N) Personnel and/or equipment certification examinations and equipment test and control records are current and available for review.	_____	_____	____
O) Maintenance checks of equipment are conducted and records maintained to verify status.	_____	_____	____

Category IV Point Average (1-100) _____

Category **IV** Notes

_____

_____

_____

_____

_____

_____

_____

_____

_____

_____

Category V. Material Storage Area, Packing, Shipping and Record Retention Control	Yes	No	Point Value
A) Acceptance for storage is based on checks for correct identification, authorized release by inspection/test, shelf life/cure data, and status of materials returned.	___	___	___
B) Storage and issue practices based on control for shelf life, cure data, engineering change status, and correct identification (color code and part, heat, job, material specification, and serial numbers).	___	___	___
C) Storage practices include control for correct location in area/bin/shelf per record, and adequate segregation and protection to prevent damage, intermingling and corrosion.	___	___	___
D) Storage and release control of materials are restricted to authorized personnel.	___	___	___
E) Evidence of acceptance status of materials and/or parts is verified prior to packaging.	___	___	___
F) Adequate material segregation, protection and handling practices are employed.	___	___	___
G) Specified material preservation practices are used.	___	___	___
H) Required enclosures are included with shipments.	___	___	___
I) Proper marking of containers is verified.	___	___	___

Category V Point Average (1-100) ___

Category V Notes

_____

_____

_____

_____

_____

_____

_____

_____

_____

_____

Category VI. Quality Program Management	Yes	No	Point Value
A) Quality control manual and/or quality procedures prescribe system requirements currently in use.	_____	_____	____
B) Quality personnel members of a professional society. Society _____ Number _____ _____ _____ _____ _____	_____	_____	____
C) Quality personnel certified (e.g. by ASQC: CQE, CRE, or CQT).	_____	_____	____
D) Philosophy regarding personnel training: In-house training.	_____	_____	____
Participation in technical courses.	_____	_____	____
Participation in college programs and/or courses.	_____	_____	____
E) Cost of quality tracked: Analysis of scrap/rework performed.	_____	_____	____
Prevention, appraisal, failure as percent of sales.	_____	_____	____
F) Internal audit performed by _____	_____	_____	____
G) Quality yield reporting.	_____	_____	____
H) Statistical yield (PPM) reported to customer.	_____	_____	____

Category VI Point Average (1-100) ____

Category VI Notes

_____

_____

_____

_____

_____

_____

_____

_____

_____

Strength Summary of System Survey

1)   Subsystem (Category) _____

     Description of Strength _____

2)   Subsystem (Category) _____

     Description of Strength _____

3)   Subsystem (Category) _____

     Description of Strength _____

4)   Subsystem (Category) _____

     Description of Strength _____

5)   Subsystem (Category) _____

     Description of Strength _____

6)   Subsystem (Category) _____

     Description of Strength _____

Use additional pages as necessary.

Corrective Action Summary for System Survey

1) Subsystem (Category) _____
   Description of Weakness _____
   _____
   _____
   _____

   Corrective Action and Date _____
   _____
   _____
   _____

2) Subsystem (Category) _____
   Description of Weakness _____
   _____
   _____
   _____

   Corrective Action and Date _____
   _____
   _____
   _____

3) Subsystem (Category) _____
   Description of Weakness _____
   _____
   _____
   _____

   Corrective Action and Date _____
   _____
   _____
   _____

4) Subsystem (Category) _____
   Description of Weakness _____
   _____
   _____
   _____

   Corrective Action and Date _____
   _____
   _____
   _____

Corrective Action Summary for System Survey (Continued)

5) Subsystem (Category) _____
   Description of Weakness _____
   _____
   _____
   _____

   Corrective Action and Date _____
   _____
   _____
   _____

6) Subsystem (Category) _____
   Description of Weakness _____
   _____
   _____
   _____

   Corrective Action and Date _____
   _____
   _____
   _____

Summary Report — Combined Rating

Category	Point Average
I. Drawing and Specification Control	_____
II. Purchased Material Control	_____
III. Measuring and Testing Equipment Control	_____
IV. Process Control and Product Acceptance	_____
V. Material Storage Area, Packing, Shipping and Record Retention Control	_____
VI. Quality Program Management	_____

$$\frac{\text{Sum of Categories 1-6}}{\text{Number of Categories}} = \text{Final Score} \qquad \text{_____}$$

---

100 = Excellent
75 = Commercial Average
50 = Unacceptable

Notes

Supplier Procurement Checklist

The attached procurement survey questionnaire often is sent to the supplier, returned and reviewed prior to placing orders, thus becoming the initial contact with the supplier. Once the process of qualifying the supplier for the Ship-to-Stock Program begins, the questionnaire should be reviewed and, if it is not current, should be updated.

Often when this questionnaire is initially sent out and returned for review, the supplier indicates that he is presently doing business with other customers in a program similar to Ship-to-Stock. This can indicate to the customer that doing business with the supplier may possibly yield even greater savings if the supplier would become an STS-qualified supplier.

Supplier Procurement Survey

Supplier Name _____

Address _____

City, State _____ Telephone _____

Reason for survey _____
_____
_____
_____

Requester of survey: Name _____
                        Title _____
                        Date _____

Approved _____ Conditional Approval _____ Disapproved _____

Supplier Procurement Survey
Part 1
Supplier Information Sheet

To establish and maintain a good business relationship with our suppliers, we ask that you complete the following:

Supplier Name _____

Address _____

City, State _____ Telephone _____

Sales Representative _____

Inside Sales Person _____

Sales Manager _____

Sales Service Manager _____

Company President _____

Address and phone number of above persons if different than above:

_____
_____
_____
_____

Product(s) sold:

_____
_____
_____
_____

Plant locations:

_____
_____
_____
_____

Do you have engineering, testing or other special service facilities that are available? What are they?

_____
_____
_____
_____

Is there a charge for these services?

_____
_____
_____
_____

Payment terms: _____
_____

FOB point: _____
_____

Method of shipment: _____
_____

Do you have your own trucks? _____
How many? _____

Special equipment you will need to produce for our requirements? _____
_____
_____
_____
_____

Do you have a union? _____

When is your contract due? _____

What is the name of your union? _____

Person completing form please sign and date.

_____
Name

_____
Title

_____
Date

Supplier Procurement Survey
Part 2
Detailed Supplier Survey

Supplier Name _____

Address _____

City, State _____ Telephone _____

Company Officers:

President _____

Vice President _____

Plant Manager _____

Treasurer _____

Sales Manager _____

QA Manager _____

Others _____

_____

_____

Prepared by: _____

         Name   Title   Survey Date

Business Information:

Individual _____ Partnership _____ Corporation _____

If not a corporation, is name of partnership legally registered? _____
_____

Subsidiary of _____
_____

Dun & Bradstreet rating _____ Report attached _____

General Information:

Total number of employees _____

Number of direct employees _____ indirect employees _____

Number of shifts _____

Type of building (wood, block, etc.) _____

Age _____ Condition of building _____

Total square footage _____ Production square footage _____

Is plant unionized? _____ Name of union _____

When does contract expire? _____

Any previous history of union strikes, etc.? _____
_____

Years in business _____

Expansion plans _____

Other manufacturing facilities? _____
Location _____

Sales Volume:

Past 3 years: Yr _____ $ _____ Yr _____ $ _____ Yr _____ $ _____

Current and projected: Yr _____ $ _____ Yr _____ $ _____ Yr _____ $ _____

Current backlog: $ _____

Lead times (weeks): Prototype: _____ Production: _____

Percent of volume allotted to military contracts: _____

List top five customers and percentage of business:

1. _____

2. _____

3. _____

4. _____

5. _____

List three major customers:

1. _____

2. _____

3. _____

List five major suppliers:

1. _____

2. _____

3. _____

4. _____

5. _____

Is the supplier currently doing business with any other customer as a Ship-to-Stock supplier?
Yes _____ No _____

1. _____

2. _____

3. _____

Would the supplier ship product to overseas facilities? Yes _____ No _____
Sales terms _____ FOB point _____

Are sales handled direct or through manufacturing representatives? _____

Type of work in which the supplier specializes _____

_____

_____

_____

Type of industry supplied _____

_____

_____

_____

Describe any unique capabilities (custom machinery, tooling, etc.). _____

_____

_____

_____

Are housekeeping and working conditions adequate? _____

_____

_____

_____

What is the condition of equipment? _____

_____

_____

_____

Does the supplier have its own product line?   Yes _____   No _____
Type _____
Square footage required _____ Number of people _____

Survey summary: List any and all limitations and/or special qualifications. Support by facilities
                      brochure where necessary.

_____
_____
_____

APPENDIX D

AUDIT GUIDELINES

Auditing is a necessary part of the Ship-to-Stock Program to ensure the continued quality of products which are shipped directly to stock. Audits are different from the Ship-to-Stock supplier surveys in that, while surveys are a preliminary evaluation of possible Ship-to-Stock candidates, audits are evaluations based on the criteria which were agreed to during qualification of the supplier quality system. Another way of looking at surveys and audits is to say that a survey is a review for system and process adequacy where an audit is a review for compliance to documented system, process and product requirements. It is my belief that these professionally conducted audits will be of benefit to both the customer and the supplier.

This appendix has been divided into the following sections.

SECTION 1   INTRODUCTION
SECTION 2   SHIP-TO-STOCK AUDIT ORGANIZATION
SECTION 3   SHIP-TO-STOCK SYSTEM AUDIT
SECTION 4   SHIP-TO-STOCK PROCESS AUDIT
SECTION 5   SHIP-TO-STOCK PRODUCT AUDIT

SECTION 1   INTRODUCTION

Ship-to-Stock audits will help ensure that the quality of products purchased through the STS Program is maintained. You and your supplier must agree to criteria relevant to three audits areas: system, process and product. Auditors will then verify, report and assure a supplier's compliance with these criteria. This appendix will define the responsibilities for auditing and provide general information for the auditing of Ship-to-Stock products.

SECTION 2   SHIP-TO-STOCK AUDIT ORGANIZATION

The Customer Representatives should handle all daily interactions with each supplier. Their auditing responsibilities should include:

- Serving as a liaison between the supplier and the customer.
- Conducting audits based on frequencies specified in the STS agreement.
- Monitoring all necessary in-house audits on STS parts.
- Documenting all audit results.
- Issuing corrective action requests when required and ensuring that they are implemented.
- Discussing audit and survey results with the supplier.
- Notifying the supplier of changes to the audit schedule.

The Supplier Representative should be responsible for the following:

- Periodically auditing his or her own company and product as specified in the STS agreement.
- Serving as a liaison between the supplier and the customer.

Scheduling and Criteria

System and process audits are based on the supplier's documentation for the system or process used to manufacture the qualified part. Product audits are based on the product's specifications for manufacture and fitness for use.

The following principles apply to all Ship-to-Stock quality audits:

- Audits should be conducted in a professional manner; nonconformances should be handled immediately in a constructive manner.
- Auditors should have a thorough knowledge of quality and auditing principles.
- Audits should be conducted "where the action is."
- The auditor should maintain control and not be led by the supplier.
- Auditors should verify all verbal information.
- Auditors should prepare an appropriate checklist before each audit emphasizing product quality and reliability. (You and your suppliers should reach a consensus on the criteria included.)
- The auditor should verify facts by informally discussing audit results with the Supplier Representative before the closing conference.
- Top management, for both the supplier and the customer, must be involved in the closing conference when the results require their attention.
- To be effective, corrective action must be followed up.
- Auditors should continually modify their checklists for successive audits to ensure the most effective audit.
- Auditors must be realistic, firm and fair.
- All audit reports should be kept on file.

Reports, including corrective action plans, should be prepared after each audit and submitted to both supplier and customer management. Formal corrective action must be taken on any critical deficiencies found during an audit. Minor deficiencies may be resolved on an informal basis, but the deficiency should be documented and corrective action verified during follow-up audits.

Ship-to-Stock Audits

System Audits

A system audit should include all phases of the supplier's system and contain six major categories:

- Drawings and specifications
- Purchased material
- Measuring and testing equipment
- Process control and product acceptance
- Storage, packing, shipping and record retention
- Quality program management

Process Audits

Process audits should be conducted periodically at the supplier's facility to ensure adherence to documentation. Usually audits are conducted quarterly to semi-annually.

Some examples of process audit frequencies are:

a. Critical products - quarterly
b. Complex, key or high volume products - quarterly
c. Minor or supplier-controlled products - semi-annually or annually.

The Customer Representative who performs process audits should establish an auditing plan that includes all phases of the supplier's process for manufacturing a particular product. The following is a list of major types of process audits shown as examples in this work.

- Machine Supplier
- Injection Molding Supplier
- Casting Supplier
- Sheet Metal or Stamping Supplier
- Special Process Audit

Product Audits

A Ship-to-Stock product audit is a review of a part to determine if it duplicates the criteria of the first article inspection. A supplier's inspection documents may also be audited during a product audit. Product audits may be conducted at the supplier's facility by either the Supplier or Customer Representative, or the audit may take place at the customer site and be performed by the Customer Representative. When the audit occurs at the supplier site and is performed by the Supplier Representative, the Customer Representative should witness or verify the process and review the results. If the audit occurs at the customer site, the auditor should use the customer's inspection areas, equipment and laboratories as needed. The Supplier Representative may be allowed to witness this process. If, the audit uncovers deficiencies, the Supplier Representative should be shown the method used. This will ensure that inspection of product is consistent regardless of where and by whom it is performed.

SECTION 3   SHIP-TO-STOCK SYSTEM AUDIT

A Ship-to-Stock system audit is an in-depth review of a supplier's system to ensure that it is in compliance with documentation. It is based on supplier standards, such as the supplier's quality manual.

System audits will usually be performed once a year or completed in sections throughout the course of the year. They will include a follow-up on corrective action areas when necessary.

System Auditing Plan

The system auditing plan is intended to include all phases of the supplier's system and contains six major categories:

1. Drawings and Specifications
2. Purchased Material
3. Measuring and Testing Equipment
4. Process Control and Product Acceptance
5. Storage, Packing, Shipping and Record Retention
6. Quality Program Management

The survey format shown in Appendix C may be used as a base from which the system audit checklists may be developed. These lists should be tailored to the supplier's system and include references to the supplier's policies and procedures where applicable.

Ship-to-Stock is considered a cooperative approach to quality. When a supplier performs an internal self audit, there is no reason why the customer auditor cannot piggy back on the information. In essence, the customer auditor can tailor his checklist to coincide with the supplier's internal audit.

The customer's auditor should complete an appropriate summary report after each audit. The auditor and the supplier's management should review the audit results and ensure that any corrective actions are implemented.

The auditor should bear in mind that the purpose of the entire audit is to evaluate a supplier's system on its ability to yield products that will not require incoming inspection at the customer's facility. Above all, everyone must remember that the audit is to *evaluate* and *improve* the audited elements if deficiency is found. The audit must be a ''win-win'' experience not a ''gotcha'' exercise.

SECTION 4   SHIP-TO-STOCK PROCESS AUDIT

A Ship-to-Stock process audit is a periodic review of the supplier's method of production and documentation of inspections to ensure that points agreed to in the Characteristic Accountability Report have been maintained. Usually process audits are conducted quarterly to semi-annually.

Some examples of process audit frequency are:

1. Critical products - quarterly
2. Complex or high volume products - quarterly
3. Minor or supplier-controlled products - semi-annually or annually

   NOTE: A breakdown indicating the frequency of audits for specific areas within each process category precedes the auditing checklist in this appendix.

The Customer Representative who performs process audits should establish an auditing plan that includes all phases of the supplier's process for manufacturing a particular product. The following pages are examples of process audits for four different supplier categories. Five special process audit checklists are also included. These checklists should be used as guidelines and may be modified to properly meet the needs of the process audit. It is important that auditors record any conditions found which are, or could be, detrimental to product quality, even if such conditions are not included on the prepared checklist.

The auditor should also complete a summary report. If necessary, the auditor and the supplier's management should review the audit results and ensure that corrective actions are implemented.

SHIP-TO-STOCK PROCESS AUDIT EXAMPLES

Major Supplier Categories

1. Machine
2. Injection Molding
3. Casting
4. Sheet Metal or Stamping

Special Process Audit Checklists

1. Painting
2. Certification Review (heat treat, plating, nondestructive testing)
3. Heat Treat
4. Plating
5. Nondestructive Testing
    X-Ray
    Penetrant

Machine Supplier Audit Example

Schedule

	Suggested
Audit Areas	Audit Frequency
A. Stock (release, traceability and storage of raw material)	Quarterly
B. Manufacturing Operations (jig boring, milling, drilling, turning, grinding, deburring, etc.)	Quarterly
C. Heat treat and plating (certification review)	Semi-annually
D. Marking	Quarterly
E. Final inspection and gauge calibration	Quarterly
F. Nondestructive testing	Quarterly
G. Plate layout	As required for first article/product audit
H. Packaging and shipping	Quarterly

Machine Supplier Process Audit

Supplier _____

Auditor _____

Date Completed _____

A. <u>Stock Area</u>   <u>Yes</u>   <u>No</u>

1. Proper paperwork is required for storage.
2. Use of stockroom is controlled.
3. Material is properly coded when going into stock.
4. Stock area is organized.
5. Material waiting testing is segregated and controlled.
6. Verification for proper alloy (lab test of certification review) occurs.
7. Material is properly coded for checkout and removed by authorized personnel only.
8. Purchase Order identifies specification, part number and revision.
9. Dimensions are verified when material is removed.

Notes

_____

_____

_____

_____

_____

_____

_____

_____

_____

_____

_____

_____

_____

_____

Machine Supplier Process Audit

Supplier _____
Auditor _____
Date Completed _____

B. Underline: Manufacturing Operations   <u>Yes</u>   <u>No</u>

    1. Area is organized.   _____ _____
    2. Measuring devices are properly calibrated.   _____ _____
    3. Received parts are properly identified.   _____ _____
    4. Drawing revisions are current.   _____ _____
    5. Detailed instructions are on or near machines.   _____ _____
    6. Operator follows instructions.   _____ _____
    7. Proper measuring equipment is available. (Refer to   _____ _____
        Characteristic Accountability Report.)
    8. Measurement of one randomly selected part corresponds to _____ _____
        dimensions on the operation sheets or engineering drawings.
    9. Dimensions generated at this station are inspected per the _____ _____
        frequency of the Characteristic Accountability Report.
   10. Discrepant parts are adequately identified and separated. _____ _____
   11. Parts sent from area are properly identified.   _____ _____

Notes

_____
_____
_____
_____
_____
_____
_____
_____
_____
_____
_____
_____
_____
_____
_____

Machine Supplier Process Audit

Supplier _____
Auditor _____
Date Completed _____

C. Certification Review (Heat Treat and Plating)   <u>Yes</u>   <u>No</u>

    1. Requirements are specified on Purchase Order.   _____   _____
    2. Proper documents are sent with part.   _____   _____
    3. Part is properly identified.   _____   _____
    4. Part is returned with proper identification.   _____   _____
    5. Part is certified to comply with specification.   _____   _____
    6. Part is tested to ensure compliance with specification. _____   _____
        Test description: _____
        _____
        _____
        _____
        _____
        _____

Notes

_____
_____
_____
_____
_____
_____
_____
_____
_____
_____
_____
_____
_____
_____
_____

Machine Supplier Process Audit

Supplier _____
Auditor _____
Date Completed _____

D. <u>Marking</u>   <u>Yes</u>   <u>No</u>

    1. Items routed to marking area are properly identified.   _____   _____
    2. Marking conforms with specified method and format.   _____   _____
    3. Specific marking instructions are available.   _____   _____
    4. Examine four part numbers for marking (size, legibility, etc.).   _____   _____

Notes

_____
_____
_____
_____
_____
_____
_____
_____
_____
_____
_____
_____
_____
_____
_____
_____

Machine Supplier Process Audit

Supplier _____
Auditor _____
Date Completed _____

	Yes	No
E. Finish Inspection and Gauge Calibration		

1. Variable dimension data are recorded and retained when required.   _____ _____
2. Dimensions and surface finish meet requirements of control drawing. (Spot check parts.)   _____ _____
3. Proper measuring equipment is available in area per Characteristic Accountability Report.   _____ _____
4. Equipment is calibrated per quality control manual. (Check records on a gauge being used.)   _____ _____
5. Inspection process sheets contain: _____ _____
   a. Characteristics to be inspected.
   b. Frequency of inspection.
   c. Gauges and fixtures to be used, if any.
6. Frequency of dimensional inspections meets minimum specified per Characteristic Accountability Report.   _____ _____
7. Inspection forms are completed properly.   _____ _____
8. Acceptable parts and paperwork are identified by inspector.   _____ _____
9. Rejected parts are tagged to distinguish them from accepted products.   _____ _____
10. Rejected parts are segregated pending disposition.   _____ _____
11. Rejected parts are reviewed at team meetings and corrective action is taken.   _____ _____

Notes

_____
_____
_____
_____
_____
_____
_____
_____
_____
_____
_____
_____
_____
_____
_____
_____
_____

Machine Supplier Process Audit

Supplier _____

Auditor _____

Date Completed _____

		Yes	No
F.	**Nondestructive Testing**		
	X-Ray		
1.	Parts that have passed X-ray inspection are marked.	_____	_____
2.	Parts are adequately deburred and cleaned to prevent false X-ray indications.	_____	_____
3.	Parts are visually inspected prior to X-ray.	_____	_____
4.	X-ray viewers are clean and located properly to ensure proper reading of film.	_____	_____
5.	X-ray technique procedure is available.	_____	_____
6.	X-rays are taken per the approved technique.	_____	_____
7.	Operator complies with the specifications of the process sheets.	_____	_____
8.	The current revision of the specification or process sheet is available.	_____	_____
9.	Proper acceptance criteria are available.	_____	_____
10.	Defects are clearly identified on parts.	_____	_____
11.	Defects are clearly identified on film.	_____	_____
12.	Records of parts inspected by X-ray are available and accurate.	_____	_____
13.	Records show accept or reject reason.	_____	_____
14.	Records are signed by the inspector.	_____	_____
15.	Discrepant parts are segregated.	_____	_____
16.	Rework parts are reviewed by engineer and routed to ensure heat treat and re-X-ray.	_____	_____
17.	Scrap material is disposed of properly.	_____	_____
18.	Film is identified with lot, part number, serial number, etc.	_____	_____
19.	Film envelope is identified.	_____	_____
20.	2T sensitivity acceptable.	_____	_____
21.	Density of film is per specification.	_____	_____
22.	Number of lots audited is per specification.	_____	_____
23.	Densitometer is available, calibrated and traceable to the National Bureau of Standards.	_____	_____
24.	The density strip is available, calibrated and traceable to the National Bureau of Standards.	_____	_____
25.	Level II/III radiographers do all acceptance reading.	_____	_____
26.	Eye examinations are current.	_____	_____
27.	Written examinations are current.	_____	_____
28.	Records of inspector's exams are available.	_____	_____
29.	Automatic processor is controlled.	_____	_____
	a. Density strips are run daily and logged.	_____	_____
	b. Temperature is checked daily.	_____	_____
	c. Replenishing rate is checked and logged periodically.	_____	_____

Machine Supplier Process Audit

		Yes	No
F.	Nondestructive Testing		

X-Ray (continued)

		Yes	No
30.	Radiographers are audited and results logged.	___	___
31.	Parts are available for review on questionable indications.	___	___
32.	Questionable parts are re-X-rayed.	___	___
33.	Film is punched with inspector identification.	___	___
34.	Certifications are properly completed.	___	___
35.	Certification identifies serial number, etc., of rejects.	___	___
36.	Film envelope or copy of certification in envelope identifies serial number of rejects.	___	___

Penetrant

		Yes	No
1.	Inspectors stamp parts that have passed penetrant inspection.	___	___
2.	Location of defect is clearly identified on part.	___	___
3.	Inspector signs records.	___	___
4.	Parts are adequately cleaned prior to penetrant inspection (scale, water, oil and grease removed).	___	___
5.	Penetrant inspection process sheet is available.	___	___
6.	The operator uses process sheet or specification.	___	___
7.	Correct revision of process sheet or specification is used.	___	___
8.	Discrepant parts are segregated.	___	___
9.	Inspectors meet eyesight requirements.	___	___
10.	Eye examinations are current.	___	___
11.	Records and test reports verify that examiners are current in certification.	___	___
12.	Parts are serialized prior to inspection.	___	___
13.	A test sample with known defects is checked to verify process.	___	___
14.	Checks for contaminations are made on penetrant, emulsifier, and developer baths or powders.	___	___
15.	Operator processing parts adheres to time cycles.	___	___

Notes

_____

_____

_____

_____

_____

_____

_____

_____

_____

_____

_____

_____

Machine Supplier Process Audit

Supplier _____

Auditor _____

Date Completed _____

G. <u>Plate Layout, First Piece</u>   <u>Yes</u>   <u>No</u>

     1.   Proper data are utilized and all characteristics are accounted for.   _____   _____

     2.   Proper tools are used.   _____   _____

     3.   All dimensions are controlled/monitored periodically.   _____   _____

Notes

_____

_____

_____

_____

_____

_____

_____

_____

_____

_____

_____

_____

_____

_____

_____

_____

Machine Supplier Process Audit

Supplier _____
Auditor _____
Date Completed _____

		<u>Yes</u>	<u>No</u>
H.	<u>Packaging and Shipping</u>		
1.	Boxes are properly labeled.	_____	_____
2.	Parts are packaged to prevent damage.	_____	_____
3.	Parts are protected against corrosion.	_____	_____
4.	X-rays are included and properly labeled when necessary.	_____	_____
5.	Packing list specifies the number of parts, test bars, and certifications enclosed.	_____	_____
6.	Release forms and certifications are enclosed as required.	_____	_____

Notes

_____
_____
_____
_____
_____
_____
_____
_____
_____
_____
_____
_____
_____
_____
_____

Machine Supplier Process Audit Summary

A) Stock Area comments: _____
_____

B) Manufacturing Operations comments: _____
_____

C) Certification Review comments: _____
_____

D) Marking comments: _____
_____

E) Final Inspection comments: _____
_____

F) Nondestructive Testing comments: _____
_____

G) Plate Layout, First Piece comments: _____
_____

H) Packaging and Shipping comments: _____
_____

General Comments: _____
_____
_____
_____
_____
_____
_____
_____
_____

Use additional pages as necessary.

Injection Molding Process Audit Example

Schedule

<table>
<tr><td>Audit Areas</td><td>Suggested
Audit Frequency</td></tr>
<tr><td>A.   Stock area (release and storage of raw material)</td><td>Quarterly</td></tr>
<tr><td>B.   Molding Operations</td><td>Quarterly</td></tr>
<tr><td>C.   Marking</td><td>Quarterly</td></tr>
<tr><td>D.   Painting</td><td>Quarterly</td></tr>
<tr><td>E.   Final inspection and gauge calibration</td><td>Quarterly</td></tr>
<tr><td>F.   Packaging and shipping</td><td>Quarterly</td></tr>
</table>

Injection Molding Process Audit

Supplier _____

Auditor _____

Date Completed _____

A. <u>Stock Area</u>   <u>Yes</u>   <u>No</u>

1. Proper coding of stock in storage.   _____ _____
2. Organized stock area.   _____ _____
3. Proper paperwork is used for stock and stock release.   _____ _____
4. Use is controlled.   _____ _____
5. Material awaiting testing is segregated and controlled.   _____ _____
6. Proper formulation certification from supplier is verified. _____ _____
7. Each batch or container leaving area is coded.   _____ _____
8. Lab that performs accept or on-site testing for uniformity of _____ _____
    granules and chemical analysis is certified.

Notes

_____

_____

_____

_____

_____

_____

_____

_____

_____

_____

_____

_____

_____

_____

_____

_____

_____

Injection Molding Process Audit

Supplier _____

Auditor _____

Date Completed _____

B. <u>Molding Operations</u>   <u>Yes</u>   <u>No</u>

   1. Drawing in use is current revision.   _____ _____

   2. Detailed instructions are on or near machines for heat, time,   _____ _____
pressure, ram speed, etc.

   3. Operator follows instructions.   _____ _____

   4. Proper measuring equipment is available per the   _____ _____
Characteristic Accountability Report.

   5. Measuring devices are properly calibrated.   _____ _____

   6. Parts periodically sampled during production run.   _____ _____

   7. Measurement of randomly selected parts or components   _____ _____
corresponds to dimensions on operations sheets or drawings.

   8. Dimensions generated are being inspected per the frequency   _____ _____
of Characteristic Accountability Report.

   9. Discrepant parts are identified and segregated.   _____ _____

  10. Parts are protected to prevent damage.   _____ _____

  11. System is in place to prevent deviations from post-molding   _____ _____
stress relief.

  12. Parts leaving area are properly identified.   _____ _____

  13. Area is organized.   _____ _____

Notes

_____

_____

_____

_____

_____

_____

_____

_____

_____

_____

_____

_____

_____

_____

Injection Molding Process Audit

Supplier _____
Auditor _____
Date Completed _____

		Yes	No
C.	Marking		

1. Material routed to area is properly identified.
2. Specified marking method and format is used.
3. Specific marking instructions are available.
4. Parts are identified for batch, material or date of molding as required.

Notes

_____
_____
_____
_____
_____
_____
_____
_____
_____
_____
_____
_____
_____
_____
_____
_____

Injection Molding Process Audit

Supplier _____
Auditor _____
Date Completed _____

D. Painting   Yes   No

   1. Paint batch has approval number.   _____   _____
   2. A current useable paint chip is available.   _____   _____
   3. The paint cycle is posted in paint area, including paint   _____   _____
       solvent mix gun pressures, bake time, temperature, etc.
   4. Equipment is in working order. Check pressure gauges, spray   _____   _____
       guns, oven charts, spray booths.
   5. Work is inspected for color, gloss and thickness.   _____   _____
   6. Work is packaged when fully dry and cool.   _____   _____

Notes

_____
_____
_____
_____
_____
_____
_____
_____
_____
_____
_____
_____
_____
_____
_____
_____
_____
_____

Injection Molding Process Audit

Supplier _____
Auditor _____
Date Completed _____

E. <u>Finish Inspection and Gauge Calibration</u>   <u>Yes</u>   <u>No</u>

1. Variable dimension data are recorded and retained when   _____ _____
   required.
2. Dimensions and surface finish meet requirements of control   _____ _____
   drawing. (Spot check parts.)
3. Proper measuring equipment is available in area per   _____ _____
   Characteristic Accountability Report.
4. Equipment is calibrated per quality control manual. (Check   _____ _____
   records on a gauge being used.)
5. Inspection process sheet contains:
   a. Characteristics to be inspected.   _____ _____
   b. Frequency of inspection.   _____ _____
   c. Gauges and fixtures to be used, if any.   _____ _____
6. Frequency of dimensional inspections meets minimum   _____ _____
   specified per Characteristics Accountability Report.
7. Finished inspection forms are completed properly.   _____ _____
8. Accepted parts and paperwork are identified by inspector.   _____ _____
9. Rejected parts are tagged and segregated pending   _____ _____
   disposition.
10. Rejected parts are reviewed at team meetings and corrective   _____ _____
    action is initiated.
11. Serial numbers or lot identification of products is inspected/   _____ _____
    recorded.
12. Accountability is possible for all products.   _____ _____
13. Physical tests such as impact and tensile are performed as   _____ _____
    required.
14. U/L flammability tests are performed as required.   _____ _____

Notes

_____
_____
_____
_____
_____
_____
_____
_____
_____
_____
_____

Injection Molding Process Audit

Supplier _____

Auditor _____

Date Completed _____

		Yes	No
F.	Packaging and Shipping		
	1. Boxes are properly labeled.	_____	_____
	2. Parts are packaged to prevent damage in transit.	_____	_____
	3. Packing list specifies number of products, test results, certifications enclosed.	_____	_____
	4. Release forms and certifications are enclosed, as required.	_____	_____

Notes

_____

_____

_____

_____

_____

_____

_____

_____

_____

_____

_____

_____

_____

_____

_____

_____

Injection Molding Process Audit Summary

A) Stock Area comments: _____

_____

B) Molding Operations comments: _____

_____

C) Marking comments: _____

_____

D) Final Inspection comments: _____

_____

E) Packaging and Shipping comments: _____

_____

F) Painting comments: _____

_____

General Comments: _____

_____

_____

_____

_____

_____

_____

_____

_____

Use additional pages as necessary.

Casting Audit Example

Schedule

Audit Areas	Suggested Audit Frequency
A. Stock (release and storage of raw material)	Quarterly
B. Molding Control	Quarterly
Investment castings (wax, assembly)	Twice Quarterly
Sand castings (pattern and mold assembly)	Twice Quarterly
C. Casting (melting and pouring)	Twice Quarterly
D. Heat Treat	Twice Quarterly
E. Material Testing (tensile, chemistry)	Quarterly
F. Marking	Quarterly
G. Final Inspection and Gauge Calibration	Quarterly
H. Nondestructive Testing (FPI, X-ray)	Quarterly
I. Finish and Straighten	Quarterly
J. Packaging and Shipping	Quarterly

Casting Process Audit

Supplier _____

Auditor _____

Date Completed _____

A. Stock (release and storage of raw material)   <u>Yes</u>   <u>No</u>

1. Proper paperwork is required for storage. _____ _____
2. Use of stockroom is controlled. _____ _____
3. Material is properly coded. _____ _____
4. Stock area is organized. _____ _____
5. Material waiting test is segregated and controlled. _____ _____
6. Verification for proper alloy (lab test of certification review) occurs. _____ _____
7. Material is properly coded for checkout and removed by authorized personnel only. _____ _____
8. Purchase Order identifies specification, part number and revision. _____ _____
9. Dimensions are verified when material is removed. _____ _____

Notes

_____
_____
_____
_____

Casting Process Audit

Supplier _____
Auditor _____
Date Completed _____

B.	Mold Control - Investment Casting	<u>Yes</u>	<u>No</u>

1. Proper identification of dies. _____ _____
2. Dies stored to prevent damage. _____ _____
3. Dimensional inspection is performed periodically on waxes _____ _____
   to verify die.
4. Detailed instructions are on or near injection mold machine, _____ _____
   including heat, time, etc.
5. Operator follows instructions. _____ _____
6. First wax inspection records are on file. _____ _____
7. Assembly procedure is documented. _____ _____
8. Photos, drawings or models of assembly are available. _____ _____
9. Waxes are properly stored. _____ _____
10. Temperature of wax area is controlled. _____ _____
11. Wax inspection is performed. _____ _____
12. Shell process instructions are in area and followed, including _____ _____
    number of dips, shell backup, dewax pressure/temperature
    and cure time.

Notes

_____
_____
_____
_____
_____
_____
_____
_____
_____
_____
_____
_____
_____
_____
_____
_____

Casting Process Audit

Supplier _____
Auditor _____
Date Completed _____

B.	Mold Control - Sand Casting	Yes	No
1.	Proper identification of pattern.	_____	_____
2.	Patterns stored to prevent damage.	_____	_____
3.	Periodic inspection to verify pattern wear.	_____	_____
4.	First part inspection from pattern on file.	_____	_____
5.	Mold procedure documented (type and condition of sand).	_____	_____
6.	Core procedure is documented.	_____	_____
7.	Mold build-up documented by photos or models showing locations of cores, chills, etc.	_____	_____
8.	Bake procedure is documented.	_____	_____
9.	Operators are following procedures.	_____	_____

Notes

_____
_____
_____
_____
_____
_____
_____
_____
_____
_____
_____
_____
_____
_____
_____
_____
_____

Casting Process Audit

Supplier _____
Auditor _____
Date Completed _____

C.   Casting (Melting and Pouring)   <u>Yes</u>   <u>No</u>

    1.   Melting instructions are in area (time, temperature, alloy   _____   _____
        additions, etc.).
    2.   Pouring instructions are in area.   _____   _____
    3.   Molders follow procedure.   _____   _____
    4.   Quality person is in area during pour.   _____   _____
    5.   Castings leaving area are properly identified.   _____   _____
    6.   Raw stock received in area is properly identified.   _____   _____
    7.   Furnace is calibrated.   _____   _____
    8.   Area is organized.   _____   _____
    9.   Scrap is properly identified.   _____   _____
  10.   Discrepant parts are segregated.   _____   _____

Notes

_____
_____
_____
_____
_____
_____
_____
_____
_____
_____
_____
_____
_____
_____
_____
_____

Casting Process Audit

Supplier _____
Auditor _____
Date Completed _____

D.   <u>Heat Treat</u>   <u>Yes</u>   <u>No</u>

1. Parts are received with proper identification.
2. Furnace is calibrated.
3. Cycle is controlled.
4. Heat treat procedures are available.
5. Procedure is being followed.
6. Furnace charts are retained.
7. Hardness is tested and recorded.
8. Area is organized.
9. Parts leaving area are properly identified.

Notes

_____
_____
_____
_____
_____
_____
_____
_____
_____
_____
_____
_____
_____
_____
_____
_____
_____

Casting Process Audit

Supplier _____
Auditor _____
Date Completed _____

E. Material Testing (Tensile and Chemistry)   <u>Yes</u>   <u>No</u>

    1. Specimen material is properly received and identified.   _____ _____
    2. Specimen is properly prepared.   _____ _____
    3. Specimen finish is proper.   _____ _____
    4. Test equipment is calibrated.   _____ _____
    5. Test is conducted per specification.   _____ _____
    6. Results are properly interpreted.   _____ _____
    7. Test results are properly documented.   _____ _____

Notes

_____
_____
_____
_____
_____
_____
_____
_____
_____
_____
_____
_____
_____
_____
_____

Casting Process Audit

Supplier _____

Auditor _____

Date Completed _____

F.	Marking	Yes	No
1.	Items routed to marking area are properly identified.	_____	_____
2.	Marking conforms with specified method and format.	_____	_____
3.	Specific marking instructions are available.	_____	_____
4.	Four part numbers are used for marking (size, legibility, etc.).	_____	_____

Notes

_____
_____
_____
_____
_____
_____
_____
_____
_____
_____
_____
_____
_____
_____
_____
_____

Casting Process Audit

Supplier _____
Auditor _____
Date Completed _____

G.	Final Inspection and Gauge Calibration	Yes	No
1.	Variable dimension data are recorded and retained when required.	_____	_____
2.	Dimensions and surface finish meet requirements of control drawing. (Spot check parts.)	_____	_____
3.	Proper measuring equipment is available in area per Characteristic Accountability Report.	_____	_____
4.	Equipment is calibrated per quality control manual. (Check records on a gauge being used.)	_____	_____
5.	Inspection process sheets contain:		
	a. Characteristics to be inspected.	_____	_____
	b. Frequency of inspection.	_____	_____
	c. Gauges and fixtures to be used, if any.	_____	_____
6.	Frequency of dimensional inspections meets minimum specified per Characteristic Accountability Report.	_____	_____
7.	Inspection forms are properly completed.	_____	_____
8.	Acceptable parts and paperwork are identified by inspector.	_____	_____
9.	Rejected products are tagged to distinguish them from accepted products.	_____	_____
10.	Rejected products are segregated pending disposition.	_____	_____
11.	Rejected products are reviewed at team meetings and corrective action is taken.	_____	_____

Notes

_____
_____
_____
_____
_____
_____
_____
_____
_____
_____
_____
_____
_____
_____
_____

Casting Process Audit

Supplier _____
Auditor _____
Date Completed _____

H.   Nondestructive Testing   <u>Yes</u>   <u>No</u>

X-Ray

1. Parts that have passed X-ray inspection are marked.   _____ _____
2. Parts are adequately deburred and cleaned to prevent false   _____ _____
   X-ray indications.
3. Parts are visually inspected prior to X-ray.   _____ _____
4. X-ray viewers are clean and located properly to ensure   _____ _____
   proper reading of film.
5. X-ray technique procedure is available.   _____ _____
6. X-rays are taken per the technique.   _____ _____
7. Operator complies with the specifications of the process   _____ _____
   sheets.
8. The current revision of the specification or process sheet is   _____ _____
   available.
9. Proper acceptance criteria are available.   _____ _____
10. Defects are clearly identified on parts.   _____ _____
11. Defects are clearly identified on film.   _____ _____
12. Records of parts that are X-ray inspected are available and   _____ _____
    accurate.
13. Records show accept or reject reason.   _____ _____
14. Records are signed by the inspector.   _____ _____
15. Discrepant parts are segregated.   _____ _____
16. Rework parts are reviewed by engineer and routed to ensure   _____ _____
    heat treat and re-X-ray.
17. Scrap material is disposed of properly.   _____ _____
18. Film is identified with lot, part number, serial number, etc. _____ _____
19. Film envelope is identified.   _____ _____
20. 2T sensitivity acceptable.   _____ _____
21. Density of film is per specification.   _____ _____
22. Number of lots audited is per specification.   _____ _____
23. Densitometer is available, calibrated and traceable to the   _____ _____
    National Bureau of Standards.
24. The density strip is available, calibrated and traceable   _____ _____
    to the National Bureau of Standards.
25. Level II/III radiographers do all acceptance reading.   _____ _____
26. Eye examinations are current.   _____ _____
27. Written examinations are current.   _____ _____
28. Records of inspector's exams are available.   _____ _____
29. Automatic processor is controlled.   _____ _____
    a. Density strips are run daily and logged.   _____ _____
    b. Temperature is checked daily.   _____ _____
    c. Replenishing rate is checked and logged periodically. _____ _____

Casting Process Audit

Supplier _____
Auditor _____
Date Completed _____

		Yes	No
H.	<u>Nondestructive Testing</u>		

X-Ray (continued)

		Yes	No
30.	Radiographers are audited and results logged.	_____	_____
31.	Parts are available for review on questionable indications.	_____	_____
32.	Questionable parts are re-X-rayed.	_____	_____
33.	Film is punched with inspector identification.	_____	_____
34.	Certifications are properly completed.	_____	_____
35.	Certification identifies serial number, etc., of rejects.	_____	_____
36.	Film envelope or copy of certification in envelope identifies serial number of rejects.	_____	_____

Penetrant

		Yes	No
1.	Inspectors stamp parts that have passed penetrant inspection.	_____	_____
2.	Location of defect is clearly identified on part.	_____	_____
3.	Inspector signs records.	_____	_____
4.	Parts are adequately cleaned prior to penetrant inspection (scale, water, oil and grease removed).	_____	_____
5.	Penetrant inspection process sheet is available.	_____	_____
6.	The operator uses process sheet or specification.	_____	_____
7.	Correct revision of process sheet or specification is used.	_____	_____
8.	Discrepant parts are segregated.	_____	_____
9.	Inspectors meet eyesight requirements.	_____	_____
10.	Eye examinations are current.	_____	_____
11.	Records and test reports verify that examiners are current in certification.	_____	_____
12.	Parts are serialized prior to inspection.	_____	_____
13.	A test sample with known defects is checked to verify process.	_____	_____
14.	Checks for contaminations are made on penetrant, emulsifier, and developer baths or powders.	_____	_____
15.	Operator processing parts adheres to time cycles.	_____	_____

Notes

_____

_____

_____

_____

_____

_____

Casting Process Audit

Supplier _____

Auditor _____

Date Completed _____

		Yes	No
I.	**Finish and Straighten**		
1.	Instructions are documented.	_____	_____
2.	Fixtures used for final acceptance are calibrated.	_____	_____
3.	Nondestructive testing is verified after straightening.	_____	_____

Notes

_____

_____

_____

_____

_____

_____

_____

_____

_____

_____

_____

_____

_____

_____

_____

Casting Process Audit

Supplier _____

Auditor _____

Date Completed _____

J.	Packaging and Shipping	Yes	No
1.	Boxes are properly labeled.	_____	_____
2.	Parts are packaged to prevent damage.	_____	_____
3.	Parts are protected against corrosion.	_____	_____
4.	X-rays are included and properly labeled when necessary.	_____	_____
5.	Packing list specifies the number of products, test bars, and certifications enclosed.	_____	_____
6.	Release forms and certifications are enclosed as required.	_____	_____

Notes

_____

_____

_____

_____

_____

_____

_____

_____

_____

_____

_____

_____

_____

_____

_____

_____

Casting Process Audit Summary

A) Stock Area comments: _____
_____

B) Mold Control comments: _____
_____

C) Casting comments: _____
_____

D) Heat Treat comments: _____
_____

E) Material Testing comments: _____
_____

F) Marking comments: _____
_____

G) Final Inspection and Gauge Calibration comments: _____
_____

H) Nondestructive Testing comments: _____
_____

I) Finish and Straighten comments: _____
_____

J) Packaging and Shipping comments: _____
_____

General Comments: _____
_____
_____
_____
_____
_____
_____
_____
_____
_____

Use additional pages as necessary.

Sheet Metal or Stampings Audit Example

Schedule

Audit Areas	Suggested Audit Frequency
A. Stock (release traceability and storage of raw material)	Quarterly
B. Manufacturing Operations (stamping, shearing, forming, welding, assembly)	Quarterly
C. Heat treat and plating (certification review)	Semi-annually
D. Marking	Quarterly
E. Finish inspection and gauge calibration	Quarterly
F. Painting	Quarterly
G. Packaging and shipping	Quarterly

Sheet Metal or Stampings Process Audit

Supplier _____
Auditor _____
Date Completed _____

A. <u>Stock Area</u>   <u>Yes</u>   <u>No</u>

1. Proper paperwork is required for storage.   _____   _____
2. Use of stockroom is controlled.   _____   _____
3. Material is properly coded.   _____   _____
4. Stock area is organized.   _____   _____
5. Material waiting test is segregated and controlled.   _____   _____
6. Verification for proper alloy (lab test of certification review) _____   _____
   occurs.
7. Material is properly coded for checkout and removed by   _____   _____
   authorized personnel only.
8. Purchase Order identifies specification, part number and _____   _____
   revision.
9. Dimensions are verified when material is removed.   _____   _____

Notes

_____
_____
_____
_____
_____
_____
_____
_____
_____
_____
_____
_____
_____
_____
_____

Sheet Metal or Stampings Process Audit

Supplier _____
Auditor _____
Date Completed _____

B. Manufacturing Operations	Yes	No
1. Parts are received with proper identification.		
2. Current revision of drawing or process sheet is used.		
3. Detailed instructions for operation are available.		
4. Operator follows instructions.		
5. Proper measuring equipment is available. (Reference the Characteristic Accountability Report.)		
6. Measuring devices are properly calibrated.		
7. Randomly selected part dimensions correspond to those found on the operation sheets or engineering drawings.		
8. Dimensions generated at this station are inspected per the frequency of the Characteristic Accountability Report.		
9. First piece from set-up was approved by QC.		
10. In-process inspections are being performed per the supplier plan.		
11. If punch, etc., was repaired during run, repair was verified by QC prior to restart.		
12. Discrepant parts are adequately identified and segregated.		
13. Parts leaving area are properly identified.		
14. Area is organized.		

Notes

_____
_____
_____
_____
_____
_____
_____
_____
_____
_____
_____
_____
_____
_____
_____
_____

Sheet Metal or Stampings Process Audit

Supplier _____

Auditor _____

Date Completed _____

C. Heat Treat and Plating (Certification Review)   <u>Yes</u>   <u>No</u>

   1. Requirements are specified on Purchase Order.   _____ _____
   2. Proper documents are sent with part.   _____ _____
   3. Part is properly identified.   _____ _____
   4. Part is returned with proper identification.   _____ _____
   5. Part is certified to comply with specification.   _____ _____
   6. Part is tested to ensure compliance with specification.   _____ _____
      Test description: _____
      _____
      _____
      _____
      _____

Notes

_____
_____
_____
_____
_____
_____
_____
_____
_____
_____
_____
_____
_____
_____
_____
_____

Sheet Metal or Stampings Process Audit

Supplier _____

Auditor _____

Date Completed _____

D. Marking <u>Yes</u>   <u>No</u>

     1. Items routed to marking area are properly identified.   _____   _____

     2. Marking conforms with specified method and format.   _____   _____

     3. Specific marking instructions are available.   _____   _____

     4. Four part numbers are used for marking (size, legibility, etc.).   _____   _____

Notes

_____

_____

_____

_____

_____

_____

_____

_____

_____

_____

_____

_____

_____

_____

_____

_____

Sheet Metal or Stampings Process Audit

Supplier _____
Auditor _____
Date Completed _____

		Yes	No
E.	Finish Inspection and Gauge Calibration		
1.	Variable dimensions data are recorded and retained when required.	_____	_____
2.	Dimensions and surface finish meet requirements of control drawing. (Spot check parts.)	_____	_____
3.	Proper measuring equipment is available in area per Characteristic Accountability Report.	_____	_____
4.	Equipment is calibrated per quality control manual. (Check records on a gauge being used.)	_____	_____
5.	Inspection process sheets contain:		
a.	Characteristics to be inspected.	_____	_____
b.	Frequency of inspection.	_____	_____
c.	Gauges and fixtures to be used, if any.	_____	_____
6.	Frequency of dimensional inspections meets minimum specified per Characteristic Accountability Report.	_____	_____
7.	Inspection forms are completed properly.	_____	_____
8.	Acceptable parts and paperwork are identified by inspector.	_____	_____
9.	Rejected products are tagged to distinguish them from accepted products.	_____	_____
10.	Rejected products are segregated pending disposition.	_____	_____
11.	Rejected products are reviewed at team meetings and corrective action is taken.	_____	_____

Notes

_____
_____
_____
_____
_____
_____
_____
_____
_____
_____
_____
_____
_____
_____
_____
_____
_____

Sheet Metal or Stampings Process Audit

Supplier _____

Auditor _____

Date Completed _____

F. <u>Painting</u>   <u>Yes</u>   <u>No</u>

1. Paint batch has approval number.   _____ _____
2. A current useable paint chip is available.   _____ _____
3. The paint cycle is posted in paint area, including paint   _____ _____
   solvent mix gun pressures, bake time, temperature, etc.
4. Equipment is in working order. Check pressure gauges, spray _____ _____
   guns, oven charts, spray booths.
5. Work is inspected for color, gloss and thickness.   _____ _____
6. Work is packaged when fully dry and cool.   _____ _____

Notes

_____

_____

_____

_____

_____

_____

_____

_____

_____

_____

_____

_____

_____

_____

_____

_____

_____

Sheet Metal or Stampings Process Audit

Supplier _____
Auditor _____
Date Completed _____

			Yes	No
G.	**Packaging and Shipping**			
	1.	Boxes are properly labeled.	———	———
	2.	Parts are packaged to prevent damage.	———	———
	3.	Parts are protected against corrosion.	———	———
	4.	X-rays are included and properly labeled when necessary.	———	———
	5.	Packing list specifies the number of products, test bars, and certifications enclosed.	———	———
	6.	Release forms and certifications are enclosed as required.	———	———

Notes

_____

_____

_____

_____

_____

_____

_____

_____

_____

_____

_____

_____

_____

_____

_____

_____

Sheet Metal or Stamping Process Audit Summary

A)   Stock Area comments: _____
_____

B)   Manufacturing Operations comments: _____
_____

C)   Heat Treat and Plating comments: _____
_____

D)   Marking comments: _____
_____

E)   Final Inspection and Gauge Calibration comments: _____
_____

F)   Painting comments: _____
_____

G)   Packaging and Shipping comments: _____
_____

General Comments: _____
_____
_____
_____
_____
_____
_____
_____
_____

Use additional pages as necessary.

Special Process Audit

Schedule

Audit Areas	Suggested Audit Frequency
A. Painting	Quarterly
B. Certification Review	Semi-annually
C. Heat Treat	Semi-annually
D. Plating	Semi-annually
E. Nondestructive Testing	Quarterly
X-Ray	
Penetrant	

Special Process Audit

Supplier _____
Auditor _____
Date Completed _____

A. Painting   Yes   No

    1. Paint batch has approval number.   _____   _____
    2. A current useable paint chip is available.   _____   _____
    3. The paint cycle is posted in paint area, including paint   _____   _____
        solvent mix gun pressures, bake time and temperature, etc.
    4. Equipment is in working order. Check pressure gauges, spray   _____   _____
        guns, oven charts, spray booths.
    5. Work is inspected for color, gloss and thickness.   _____   _____
    6. Work is packaged when fully dry and cool.   _____   _____

Notes

_____
_____
_____
_____
_____
_____
_____
_____
_____
_____
_____
_____
_____
_____
_____

Special Process Audit

Supplier _____
Auditor _____
Date Completed _____

B. <u>Certification Review</u>   <u>Yes</u>   <u>No</u>

1. Requirements are specified on Purchase Order.   _____ _____
2. Proper documents are sent with part.   _____ _____
3. Part is properly identified.   _____ _____
4. Part is returned with proper identification.   _____ _____
5. Part is certified to comply with specification.   _____ _____
6. Part is tested to ensure compliance with specification.   _____ _____
   Test description: _____
   _____
   _____
   _____
   _____
   _____

Notes

_____
_____
_____
_____
_____
_____
_____
_____
_____
_____
_____
_____
_____
_____
_____

Special Process Audit

Vendor _____
Auditor _____
Date Completed _____

C.	Heat Treat	Yes	No
1.	Proper documents are sent with parts.	_____	_____
2.	Parts are properly identified.	_____	_____
3.	Returned parts are properly identified.	_____	_____
4.	The area is organized.	_____	_____
5.	The flow of material is controlled.	_____	_____
6.	Check the furnace control and calibration.	_____	_____
7.	Heat treat instructions are available and identify the following:		
a.	Furnace type	_____	_____
b.	Load pattern	_____	_____
c.	Preheat treat cleaning	_____	_____
d.	Preheat time and temperature	_____	_____
e.	Solution time and temperature	_____	_____
f.	Quench medium	_____	_____
g.	Quench medium temperature	_____	_____
h.	Age time and temperature	_____	_____
i.	Cleaning method	_____	_____
j.	Special instructions	_____	_____
k.	Hardness test, etc., is recorded.	_____	_____
l.	Furnace charts are retained.	_____	_____

Notes

_____
_____
_____
_____
_____
_____
_____
_____
_____
_____
_____
_____
_____
_____
_____
_____

Special Process Audit

Vendor _____

Auditor _____

Date Completed _____

D. Plating   Yes   No

1. Parts are received with proper identification.
2. The cleaning process is being followed.
3. The cleaning process is under control.
4. The plating process cycle is available in the area.
5. The plating process is being followed.
6. Accept/reject criteria establish specifications, thickness, sampling, etc.
7. Temperature instruments are calibrated.
8. Solutions are checked periodically and recorded.
9. Solutions are re-analyzed after additions of chemicals.
10. Materials used for solutions are certified or a chemical analysis is performed.
11. Plated parts are baked after plate to relieve hydrogen embattlement as required.
12. Finished parts inspection record is available.
13. Parts are protected to prevent handling damage.
14. Defective parts are segregated and removed for material review.
15. Certification is provided and traceable to lot or batch.
16. Area is organized.

Notes

_____
_____
_____
_____
_____
_____
_____
_____
_____
_____
_____
_____
_____
_____

Special Process Audit

Vendor _____

Auditor _____

Date Completed _____

E. <u>Nondestructive Testing</u>   <u>Yes</u>   <u>No</u>

X-Ray

1. Parts that have passed X-ray inspection are marked. _____ _____
2. Parts are adequately deburred and cleaned to prevent false X-ray indications. _____ _____
3. Parts are visually inspected prior to X-ray. _____ _____
4. X-ray viewers are clean and located properly to ensure proper reading of film. _____ _____
5. X-ray technique procedure is available. _____ _____
6. X-rays are taken per the approved technique. _____ _____
7. Operator complies with the specifications of the process sheets. _____ _____
8. The current revision of the specification or process sheet is available. _____ _____
9. Proper acceptance criteria is available. _____ _____
10. Defects are clearly identified on parts. _____ _____
11. Defects are clearly identified on film. _____ _____
12. Records of parts inspected by X-ray are available and accurate. _____ _____
13. Records show accept or reject reason. _____ _____
14. Records are signed by the inspector. _____ _____
15. Discrepant parts are segregated. _____ _____
16. Rework parts are reviewed by engineer and routed to ensure heat treat and re-X-ray. _____ _____
17. Scrap material is disposed of properly. _____ _____
18. Film is identified with lot, part number, serial number, etc. _____ _____
19. Film envelope is identified. _____ _____
20. 2T sensitivity acceptable. _____ _____
21. Density of film is per specification. _____ _____
22. Number of lots audited is per specification. _____ _____
23. Densitometer is available, calibrated and traceable to the National Bureau of Standards. _____ _____
24. The density strip is available, calibrated and traceable to the National Bureau of Standards. _____ _____
25. Level II/III radiographers do all acceptance reading. _____ _____
26. Eye examinations are current. _____ _____
27. Written examinations are current. _____ _____
28. Records of inspector's exams are available. _____ _____
29. Automatic processor is controlled. _____ _____
    a. Density strips are run daily and logged. _____ _____
    b. Temperature is checked daily. _____ _____
    c. Replenishing rate is checked and logged periodically. _____ _____

Special Process Audit

F. Nondestructive Testing   Yes   No

X-Ray (continued)

30. Radiographers are audited and results logged.   _____ _____
31. Parts are available for review on questionable indications.   _____ _____
32. Questionable parts are re-X-rayed.   _____ _____
33. Film is punched with inspector identification.   _____ _____
34. Certifications are properly completed.   _____ _____
35. Certification identifies serial number, etc., of rejects.   _____ _____
36. Film envelope or copy of certification in envelope identifies _____ _____
    serial number of rejects.

Penetrant

1. Inspectors stamp parts that have passed penetrant inspection. _____ _____
2. Location of defect is clearly identified on part.   _____ _____
3. Inspector signs records.   _____ _____
4. Parts are adequately cleaned prior to penetrant inspection   _____ _____
    (scale, water, oil and grease removed).
5. Penetrant inspection process sheet is available.   _____ _____
6. The operator uses process sheet or specification.   _____ _____
7. Correct revision of process sheet or specification is used.   _____ _____
8. Discrepant parts are segregated.   _____ _____
9. Inspectors meet eyesight requirements.   _____ _____
10. Eye examinations are current.   _____ _____
11. Records and test reports verify that examiners are current in _____ _____
    certification.
12. Parts are serialized prior to inspection.   _____ _____
13. A test sample with known defects is checked to verify   _____ _____
    process.
14. Checks for contaminations are made on penetrant, emulsifier,   _____ _____
    and developer baths or powders.
15. Operator processing parts adheres to time cycles.   _____ _____

Notes

_____
_____
_____
_____
_____
_____
_____
_____
_____
_____

Special Process Audit Summary

A) Painting comments: _____

_____

B) Certification Review comments: _____

_____

C) Heat Treat comments: _____

_____

D) Plating comments: _____

_____

E) Nondestructive Testing comments: _____

_____

General comments: _____

_____
_____
_____
_____
_____
_____

Use additional pages as necessary.

SECTION 5   SHIP-TO-STOCK PRODUCT AUDIT

A Ship-to-Stock product audit is a review of a part to determine if it meets the criteria of the specification much in the same way as was done with the first article inspection or qualification. Product audits may be conducted at the supplier's site by either the Supplier or Customer Representative, or the audit may take place at the customer site and be performed by the Customer Representative. When the audit is performed by the Supplier at the supplier's site, the Customer Representative should witness or verify the process and review the data collected. If the audit occurs at the customer site, the auditor should use the customer's inspection areas, equipment and laboratories as required. The Supplier Representative may choose to witness this process.

Product Auditing Plan

A product audit should be conducted after all processes and inspections have been completed. Since the purpose is to determine if the supplier's process manufactures a product which meets established specifications, the audit should consist of checking all parameters, including dimensions, material certifications, and, where applicable, certifications of nondestructive or reliability tests. Using product standards, drawings and specification listings, the auditor should list all of the elements of the part that must be audited. In essence, a product audit is like doing another first article inspection. The results of the audit will verify that the previously agreed-to process still produces product that meets specification.

The auditor should complete a summary report for every product audit which will be kept on file. The auditor and the supplier's management should review the audit results and, if necessary, ensure that corrective action is implemented.

Product Audit Scheduling

Product audits are conducted based on time or on quantity. For example, the audit could be conducted monthly or quarterly, or for every 20,000 pieces shipped. The frequency must be agreed to in the Ship-to-Stock Agreement. If a part is scheduled to be audited but will not be shipped during a particular month, the very next shipment should be audited. If a supplier has many similar parts in the program, a randomly chosen part from a family of parts should be audited.

APPENDIX E

HOW TO COMPLETE
THE CHARACTERISTIC ACCOUNTABILITY REPORT

Block	Title	Responsibility	Action
1	Drawing Number	Customer	Enter the number of the drawing or specification on which the part appears. When a drawing is not available or does not exist, enter N/A.
2	Revision	Customer	Enter the revision level of the drawing listed in Block 1.
3	Part Number	Customer	Enter the customer part number.
4	Revision	Customer	Enter the revision level of the part in Block 3.
5	Part Number	Supplier	Enter the supplier part number.
6	Revision	Supplier	Enter the revision level of the part in Block 5.
7	Part Description	Customer	Enter a brief description of the part being considered.
8	Product Line	Customer	Enter the product line in which the part will be used.
9	Supplier Name	Customer	Enter the name of the supplier being considered for the STS Program.
10	Address	Customer	Enter the address of the supplier listed in Block 9.
11	Item	Customer	Enter the items that are to be considered for evaluation, beginning with number 01 and continuing 02, 03, etc., until all critical and major characteristics have been listed.
12	Characteristic Class	Customer	Enter the class of the characteristics, using the MIS-STD-105 criteria (critical, major, minor and cosmetic).
13	Characteristic and Tolerance	Customer	Enter each characteristic necessary to fully describe the STS candidate part and indicate width of tolerance on that part. For example, characteristics on paint might include color, thickness, durability and finish.
14	Drawing Location	Customer	Enter the location of the characteristic on the drawing.
15	Process/Machine	Supplier	Indicate the process or machine that will be used to manufacture the part characteristic.
16	Point of Control	Supplier	Indicate where in the manufacturing process the characteristic will be inspected or audited.
17	Method Measured	Supplier	List the testing or inspection method(s) and equipment used to determine whether the process producing the listed characteristic is in control.
18	Frequency of Inspection	Supplier	Enter the Acceptable Quality Level (AQL) and/or the frequency of inspection.
19	Remarks	Customer/ Supplier	Enter any additional comments referenced by line item.

Block	Title	Responsibility	Action
20	Prepared by	Customer	Engineer in the customer's organization who completed the report.
21	Approved by	Customer	The Customer Representative responsible for the part being qualified will sign and date this block.
22	Completed by	Supplier	The Supplier Representative responsible for the part being qualified will sign and date this block.
23	Approved by	Customer	The customer STS Program Manager will sign and date this block.

SHIP-TO-STOCK CHARACTERISTIC ACCOUNTABILITY REPORT

Customer Drawing No. ①	Rev.②	Product Line ⑧
Customer Part No. ③	Rev.④	Supplier Name ⑨
Supplier Part No. ⑤	Rev.⑥	Address ⑩
Part Description ⑦		

Item	Class	Characteristic* and Tolerance	B/P Loc.	Process/ Machine	Point of Control (In-Process/ Final/Etc.)	Method Measured	Frequency of Insp. (AQL %)
⑪	⑫	⑬	⑭	⑮	⑯	⑰	⑱

*NOTE: All Critical Product Characteristics must be accounted for.

Remarks: ⑲

| Prepared by - Customer ⑳ Date | Completed by - Supplier ㉒ Date |
| Appr. by - Customer Rep. ㉑ Date | Appr. by - Cust. STS Program Mgr. ㉓ Date |

Sheet _____ of _____

Figure 14

Index